Group Leadership

Strategies for Group Counseling Leaders

Third Edition

Marguerite R. Carroll
Professor Emeritus
Fairfield University

Marilyn M. Bates
late of California State
University, Fullerton

Clarence D. Johnson
Management Consultant
Irvine, California

LOVE PUBLISHING COMPANY®
Denver • London • Sydney

Published by Love Publishing Company
Denver, Colorado 80222

Library of Congress Catalog Card Number 95-082150

Printed in the U.S.A.
ISBN 0-89108-249-2

The third edition of this book is dedicated to the late Marilyn Bates who, in the early 1970s, gave us the constructs for the "Extensional Model." Her commitment to humanity lives through her publications as well as through those who worked with her in the many areas of her daily life. As a self-recognized student of life and as a professionally recognized contributor to counseling, Marilyn influenced great numbers of people directly and indirectly.

M. R. Carroll

C. D. Johnson

Contents

3   Patterns of Interaction: Individual Behavior   35
in the Group

4   Leader Techniques: The Basics   49

5   Developing Good Group   63
Communication Skills

6   Pathways to Leadership   83

7 Co-Leadership Issues   97

8 Working with Difficult Group Members   105

9 Verbal and Nonverbal Activities to   123
Promote Interaction

10 The Extensional Group Model in   149
School Settings

Preface

The central organizing principle of this book is founded in existential philosophy, a principle that has endured over time. The extensional model is based on a "well" model, whereby the expression of feelings, the search for self-knowledge, the examination of self, the desire for interaction, and the commitment to self-growth are the substance of participation. The extensional model is appropriate for use in institutional settings as diverse as elementary and secondary schools, probation departments, mental health units, and group settings outside of institutions, such as marriage and family counseling groups, community groups, rehabilitation groups, and group offerings in private practice.

The basic premise of this book is that open, honest, direct communication among human beings is both possible and desirable. Socially closed, inhibited, and self-protective styles of interpersonal behavior often seem more common, but such interpersonal styles can become more debilitating and possibly emotionally injurious than expected. It is assumed that group leaders, through good training and a commitment to excellence, can be directed toward maintaining a group environment in which members are willing, if not eager, to risk self-disclosure and to reveal their thoughts, feelings, and reactions as they are experiencing them. In such an environment, group members are more inclined to relate to each other as genuine persons rather than with a protective facade; consequently, group members feel relatively less inhibited with less need to be defensive. Interaction of this nature is not only the goal of the group leader but is the substance and essence of the extensional group process. Interaction is most beneficial when it is spontaneous and without pretext, as both educational and therapeutic benefits can be gained. The result is that individual group members will learn new ways of perceiving themselves and others.

Groups can be for better or worse. While it is inconceivable that a leader would deliberately set out to form a group for worse, participants may approach groups anticipating one type of experience and find something quite different. A high probability exists that many people who could use group process for positive growth avoid getting involved for fear of a destructive experience. In the hands of an adequately trained leader, participants need not fear and can anticipate positive growth. Competent leaders are the key.

Training group leaders to handle positive group processes is the focus of this book. Such training involves both theory and practice. The group model that provides the conceptual framework for this manual is the *extensional group*. The philosophical foundation of the extensional group—existentialism—is featured. Selected concepts of this philosophy are applied to the extensional group model. Chapters 1 and 2 interpret the philosophical and theoretical framework of the model. The remaining chapters describe the practice derived from the philosophy and theory.

The extensional group is typified as a self-actualizing group, which is based on a developmental conceptualization and is motivated primarily by the growth needs of members. Other kinds of groups (for example, task groups, support and self-help groups, guidance groups) may have a different focus and yet may have some of the characteristics of extensional group work described in this book. Chapter 3 focuses on the patterns of group interaction that can occur. Chapters 4, 5, 6, and 9 concentrate on the techniques and strategies of the leader of extensional groups. Chapter 7 discusses the advantages and disadvantages of co-leadership. Chapter 8 offers helpful ways for the leader to deal with difficult members. Chapter 11 presents the ways of training group leaders. Typical group settings are described briefly in Chapter 1 and in greater detail in Chapter 10.

Introducing the
Extensional Model

From the Past to the Present

When the "far out" anti-estab-lishment movement was attracting so much negative attention during the late 1960s and early 1970s, group work began to receive some "bad press." With an unpopular war, civil rights marches, assassinations, and moon walks monopolizing our attention, we were in a period of incredibly rapid societal and value changes, and much confusion resulted. Group work was often maligned and misinterpreted as contributing to social unrest. Thus, some conservatives were suspicious of, if not openly hostile to, group work.

It is true that in a large segment of our society groups did acquire a faddish mystique that often attracted incompetent leaders and participants who were looking for miraculous psychological cures, instant intimacy, and personal growth.

A "groupie" cult began to emerge that not only distracted from spontaneous group interaction but also fostered the antithesis of independence and self-responsibility that group work is supposed to promote.

Sleepless weekend marathons, nude encounter groups, group massages, and reports of promiscuous sex made titillating copy for media coverage a few decades ago. Indeed, some bizarre, irresponsible, and sometimes harmful things were going on in the name of group work and personal growth. Such irresponsibility fueled the questions and suspicions of those who wished to disparage group work and, in one case at least, any form of group work was automatically categorized as part of the Communists' efforts to brainwash and misguide the youth of our nation (Allen, 1968). Highly respected group researchers tried to sort out the good from the bad, the effective from the ineffective (Lieberman, Yalom, & Miles, 1973), only to be criticized by researchers of equally respected stature. During the late 1960s and early 1970s few people were neutral about group work. It was a period of vigorous debate on many issues, including the actual authority of group participation.

Becoming a participant in a new group still provokes moist palms and an accelerated heart rate. The unknown element associated with getting to know others and allowing ourselves to be known by others is an exhilarating phenomenon. It starts the adrenalin flowing, and in some cases it can be disquieting and evoke fear. These types of reactions, which also occur in nongroup situations, compound the negative public attitudes toward group work. Fortunately, those negative attitudes have mellowed. The increasing number and variety of group settings attest to the fact that groups no longer create the suspicions and the intense reaction that they once did.

To illustrate the increasing interest and acceptance of group work, this book provides an overview of the multiple settings in which group participation has become an important part of personal growth and development. Presented generically, the overview reflects the range of purposes and situations in which the extensional group model has been applied. Not all of the groups described in the chapters that follow use the term *extensional* or follow the concepts it embodies. We advocate this model, however, because it has a unique potential for effectiveness and flexibility in both extensional and therapy groups.

Differences Between Extensional and Psychotherapy Groups

Much confusion seems to exist about groups formed for what is essentially the remediation of inadequate personal functioning (therapy groups) and groups formed to extend adequate personality functioning (extensional groups). Ill people need to get better. Well people also can get better. Psychotherapy or therapy groups are concerned with ill persons who are not currently coping with the stresses and strains of living. The group leader conducting a therapy group may find that members must regress before they can mobilize themselves toward positive experiences.

Many group leaders have believed that all groups must regress to more primitive forms of behavior before growth is possible. Traditionally, such leaders have assumed that all members must discharge energies connected with experiences that, for example, may be charged with hate, fear, or anger. That regression is necessary and appropriate in therapy groups is recognized. Groups composed of members who need to repair personality defects must scrape off layers of debilitating defense mechanisms before the core personality can be restructured even minimally. Thus, an underlying thesis of the therapy group is that a person's discomfort cannot change for the better until it is confronted honestly, rather than projecting blame on others or justifying present disruptive behavior.

Not all groups are primarily for ill people, entailing a regressive, acting-out, remedial process. Groups can serve another function, extending the life-space of members by extending their capabilities—even if they are currently functioning at a satisfactory or even a self-actualizing level of existence. This particular use of groups has often been confused with the therapeutic use of groups, but different procedures and different assumptions apply to therapy groups and extensional groups.

The extensional group focuses on the concept that people who are functioning adequately, who are fairly comfortable in their interpersonal relationships, and who may be coping well with the demands of daily living can still experience growth in a self-actualizing paradigm. Although members of this type of group are "well" rather than "ill," they want to expand their personal development. They want to enhance their learning ability and attain more enjoyment from living by increasing their spontaneity, creativity, autonomy, and productivity. They want to be more aware and accepting of themselves and others and more accepting of necessary restrictions. In short, they want to accelerate the process of self-actualization. The extensional group provides an opportunity for members to explore more satisfying ways of behaving in relation to themselves and in relation to one another. The extensional model is developmental rather than remedial, extensional rather than regressive. The leader does not assume that negative forces must be uprooted before positive forces can be manifested.

The therapy group is conceptualized as dealing with potentially disruptive content, such as anger toward authority figures, resentment of early experiences, and debilitating defense mechanisms—in general, behaviors that are primarily based in a more primitive ego state. Thus, the content of the group interaction may focus on potentially destructive elements. But extensional and therapy groups overlap to some extent. The therapy group does process positive forces, although the leader is alert at all times to negative content and impact. And the extensional group deals with some negative content, but for the most part it has a predisposition for attending to the positive forces present.

In either group setting, therapy or extensional, the success of the group's interaction depends on the degree of trust, openness, and interpersonal risk-taking among the group members. Members who reveal little of themselves cannot be expected to benefit from their group experience to the same extent as members who are open and sharing.

Major Elements of Extensional Groups

When we look at the people and events around us—even when we look at ourselves in the mirror—we can never escape the possibility that what we see is a subjective view filtered through a storehouse of past experiences. Hearing from others about their perceptions and observations can confirm or contradict what we think we already know. Their sharing can give us bits of information of which we may have been unaware, all contributing to a more clearly defined picture of who and what we are and the kinds of options offered by people and events around us. Those who desire a clearer, more accurate picture of themselves have an opportunity to focus on the self and on their personal value system in an extensional group. Participating in the interaction of the group affords us an opportunity to explore the question: "Are my expressed values consistent with my behaviors?" Feedback from fellow group members can give us information we might not otherwise have access to. Among the elements necessary for self-exploration are the ability to self-disclose, authentic behavior, personal risk-taking, and balancing personal privacy and risk. These elements are discussed next.

Self-Disclosure

> *So often, that which we are is sacrificed to that which we wish ourselves to be.*
>
> (Anglund, 1970)

Why do many of us seem to be so inhibited, protective, and defensive about disclosing our present (here-and-now) feelings to each other? Powell (1969) asks a provocative question in his book: *Why Am I Afraid to Tell You Who I Am?* He discusses at length what impedes us in getting close to another person. How many of us can truthfully deny that we spend a good part of our lives trying to be the kind of person we think we *ought* to be rather than the kind of person we really *are?* Think of that for a moment. So many roles are expected of us, so many roles that we are obliged to fulfill. We are fathers, mothers, friends, neighbors, teachers, counselors, students, and affiliates of organizations and churches. We believe that certain behaviors and attitudes are expected of us as part of the roles in which we are engaged. That is the way of life.

We do not suggest that expected roles are inappropriate or undesirable. On the contrary, to be contributing members of society we must be conscious of the need for our roles as a part of family, school, community, and nation. But we are often inclined to *play* roles rather than be ourselves as a part of the roles. You can probably recall events in your life when you were so conscious of the roles in which you were functioning that you knowingly suppressed your own thoughts and attitudes to maintain the image you perceived to be consistent with your role. A good example of this is the teacher who struggles through an answer to a student's question when the most honest response would be "I don't know" or "I'm not certain."

Authentic Behavior

> *The soul selects her own society.*
>
> (Emily Dickinson)

We often present a "front," or facade, that we want others to see and believe. We adjust our behavior in a way we think is consistent with the image we wish to convey. Often the facade does not match our feelings and our true attitudes. At these times there is an incongruency between our presented self and our "real" self. When our presented self and our real self are reasonably congruent, we can think of ourselves as being *authentic*.

The difference between the presented self and the real self is far more complex than the simple dichotomy described so far. Depending on the environment we are in or the company around us, we vary in our willingness and ability to be authentic. A helpful way of conceptualizing the complexity of our varying degrees of authenticity is to think of the structural characteristics of an onion. The outer layer of an onion is quite different in texture and color from the layers near the center. As each layer is peeled away, a tender, more vulnerable surface is exposed. In our personalities our facades are often a protection for what we consider the more vulnerable and sensitive yet more real and authentic parts of ourselves.

Behavior is authentic when what we say and do is congruent with what we are really thinking and feeling. This, of course, is clearly a matter of degree rather than a state of being. When we say that someone is authentic or genuine, we mean that they seem authentic and genuine most of the time we are with them. Even the most authentic people, however, find it expedient sometimes not to disclose exactly what they are thinking or feeling.

Personal Risk-Taking

The art of a warrior is to balance the terror of being a man with the wonder of being a man.

(Carlos Castaneda)

The leader's function is to exert an influence on the group's environment that will free members to trust each other enough to open themselves and let themselves be known to each other. If the leaders are successful in helping dissolve or moving through defensive facades, the group goal of personal growth for group members should be accomplished.

John Wallen, in his article "The Constructive Use of Feelings" (n.d.), asks his readers to engage in an experiment over the course of several days. The task is to examine the way in which people talk about feelings. Expressions like "Now let's keep our feelings out of this" or "You shouldn't feel that way" are certainly common experiences for people engaged in problem-solving dialogue. Crying often prompts a response like "Don't cry," "You'll feel better," "Cheer up," or "It's ridiculous to feel that way." An expression of anger might be met with the admonishment, "You're letting your feelings get the best of you," or the assertion, "You can't behave like that."

These statements surely indicate an attitude about feelings that is familiar to us all. When we understand that some people are naturally unaccustomed to or uncomfortable about dealing directly with reports of their feelings and the feelings of others, we become sensitive to the delicate balance of the group dy-namic process. In this process, with its underlying assumption that self-disclosure is an essential condition for developing self-awareness, we encourage group members to risk that which they have learned to protect so well.

Balancing Personal Privacy and Risk

If we are to proceed into this protected life-space, we must take care not to violate that which is private and personal. As lead-ers or members of a group, we must recognize that one of the most cherished and sacred rights within our society is that of privacy. Humankind has waged both personal and general battle to protect this right. A person whose private space is invaded usually reacts as would a nation whose boundaries have been attacked. In many ways the life-space we protect is analogous to territorial boundaries that animals protect. When our privacy is violated, we react defensively. Thus, it is essential within the group setting to be sensitive to a members' private worlds and to allow them to maintain privacy if they choose to do so.

This maxim appears easy to respect—deceptively so. In pur-suit of the dynamic upon which group counseling is based (shar-ing of self), invasion of privacy becomes a tempting modus operandi not only for the leader but for other members as well. All too often in our zeal to pursue members' inner feelings, trying to help them express themselves in hopes that they will learn more about themselves, we use probing and pressure to force self-disclosure rather than allowing it to happen. As a result, members whose personal spaces have been violated are likely to react defensively, either by investing more in maintaining their facades or by withdrawing and becoming more inhibited and guarded. Individuals who feel their privacy being invaded will be unwilling to venture outside the protective barrier.

Guaranteeing members' rights to privacy is founded on our respect for the individual. On the basis of our experience in group work with adults and children, we maintain that personal risk is essential for development of self-awareness, but, ironically, the concept of risk usually raises images of intrusion or attack from the outside. One of the group leader's primary functions is to protect individual member's rights. When group members feel certain that the group milieu will be "safe," they will be more inclined to emerge from their defensive posture and share their here-and-now experiences.

Extensional Group Settings

Before proceeding to Chapter 2, in which the philosophical base of extensional groups is examined, it might be helpful to consider briefly the types of groups that seem to benefit from this approach. Although the philosophical base influences several common aspects of leader conduct and use of facilitative techniques, the group setting and the specific group purpose dictate the appropriateness and intensity of participant interaction. Not *all* techniques and *all* degrees of interaction intensity are appropriate for *all* types of extensional groups. Furthermore, group leaders may not be aware of the extensional model and, therefore, do not identify their approach as such. The various group settings to be described are, by design, neither guidance groups nor therapy groups. Thus, by our definition, they can be described as extensional groups because the processes and techniques employed are intended to help individuals capitalize on the growth potential they already possess. Details of group organization and suggestions for appropriate techniques are discussed in later chapters. Here, we wish to provide only a brief overview of the wide range of settings in which extensional groups have proved beneficial.

Educational Settings

The mention of "group" work among educators at one time automatically triggered negative feelings and resistance. This reaction was partly a carryover effect from a time when group experience usually meant something on the order of sensitivity or encounter groups. Verbal assaults on group members and attempts to strip away psychological defenses were frightening prospects that seemed to characterize popular conceptions of group experience.

Extensional groups can be used effectively as an educational procedure. At all levels of education, teachers, instructors, and professors are expressing a growing interest in finding ways to assist students in developing interpersonal skills and improving learning. For example, groups usually focus on issues of self-esteem, peer pressure, decision making, alienation, and interpersonal skills. Krieg (1988) states, "the focus is prevention, not crisis intervention or treatment" (p. 9). And Trotzer (1989) as well recognizes that those participating in counseling groups (sometimes called process groups) learn skills that encourage interpersonal interaction, discussion, and sharing, which in turn "help group members understand themselves, their development, and their world" (p. 342).

In addition to counseling or process groups, Johnson and Johnson (1995) describe content groups in which those participating expect to learn specific content and to acquire the same set of competencies. These groups are discussed in more detail in Chapter 10.

The extensional model provides an effective framework for implementing academic and nonacademic concerns, although age, maturity, and grade level will determine how the model is implemented.

Community Settings

Women's groups, senior citizens' groups, juvenile probation groups, after-care groups, and drug and alcohol rehabilitation groups are examples of the types of community groups in which extensional group work can be effective. A group environment is provided in which individuals state their views and then receive feedback, suggestions, and ideas from peers.

Medical Settings

The growing interest in holistic health encompasses the idea that patients can influence the outcome of their own medical conditions. Whether the medical setting is intended for temporary or chronic patients and their families, the type of group interaction encouraged from the extensional model can be helpful in reducing the sense of isolation and fear.

Discovering that others suffer from a similar affliction or condition decreases the "why me?" feeling. Receiving support and suggestions from those who truly understand as a result of their situations adds a richer dimension to empathy. Traditionally, group work conducted in medical settings has been exclusively remedial. Now, the emerging interest in group work for holistic health purposes is new and exciting.

Summary

Chapter 1 introduced the extensional (growth) model for group work and contrasted it with the psychotherapy (therapy) model. The extensional model focuses on what is "right" about an individual rather than trying to correct something that has gone "wrong." A basic assumption of the extensional model is that benefits derived from self-disclosure and subsequent feedback from group members will encourage self-responsibility and personal development.

The group, influenced by competent leadership, is a unique and safe environment for self-disclosure. Self-disclosure should always be a member's choice, and the leader has a responsibility to protect each member's right to privacy. Even though the model stresses the importance of self-disclosure, it is equally important that the member choose to self-disclose.

Chapter 1 also included a brief preview of various group settings—educational, community, and medical—in which the extensional model is known to have been effective.

2

The Philosophical
Base of the
Extensional
Group Model

The philosophical foundation of the extensional group is the *existentialist* framework. The implications of existentialism for individual counseling relationships have been discussed elsewhere (Bates & Johnson, 1969; Dreyfus, 1962). Our purpose in the following pages is to specify the implications of an existentialist stance for leaders of extensional groups.

The massive proliferation of groups today is a result of the alienation, loss of purpose, impersonalization, and dehumanization that all seem part of the *zeitgeist* of our times. If it is true that a particular philosophy reflects the *zeitgeist* of each age, the philosophy of existentialism most certainly reflects the anguish of mid-century humankind as we despair of "Truth" in a shattered world. The search for meaning, for encounter, for I-Thou, confirmation of a universal *angst* as a basic condition, facing the loneliness of responsible choices—all these thread contemporary thought, and they have profound implications for the leader of an extensional group.

Many people perceive the existentialist philosophy as obscure and Godless, redundant and solipsistic, reactionary and anti-establishment. Others who have struggled with the convolutions of existentialist thought have found ideas that are lucid, spiritual, challenging, and comforting. Internalizing the concepts of this philosophy often has been, for those who persevere, an intense and personal experience. Group leaders who work from within an existentialist framework find that leading a group is an intense and personal experience.

The concepts of existentialism relevant to group processes are articulated here in the first person since they are highly personal statements. The implications for leaders of extensional groups are delineated for each concept. Illustrative dialogues are provided where appropriate.

Existence Precedes Essence

A World Without Givens. I find myself thrown into a world void of all prior meaning. I find that I have arrived on the scene of life without a road map of the territory. I know one and only one certainty—death. Nothing else from this time on is a "given." No script has been written that I can consult. I am given no models, no "grand designs," no assurance that there is a teleological carpet that unfolds as I move toward death. I am on my own—alone.

I know that I exist. Now I must define myself and try to make meaning out of this world without meaning. I am completely free because there is no a priori. I am faced with the task of creating my world, which offers limitless possibilities without pre-established requirements. I exist. I find myself free to define my essence, and however I choose to define myself is up to me. I know that my statement concerning my essence will be unique, just as everyone's is unique. I know that I am different from any human being who ever lived before me or who ever will live after me, and I conceive of myself as fluid rather than static, moving rather than still, evolving rather than evolved, never finished.

My Signature of Essence. So I find that I am my own essence-giver. My life is an unanswered question to be answered however I choose. There are many times when I cry for the security of someone who will define me in the morass of this dreadful ambiguity, where all the certainty I have available is that at the end of my defining, death awaits. I know that I will be flung back into another unknown, perhaps like the unknown from which

I was flung, but this time the unknown is ahead of me, an anticipation rather than a residual memory—and a certainty.

Between this terrible nothing and the unknown to come I must make a statement concerning my essence. I am filled with angst because of the unknowns that dwell on either side of me. I cry for the security of givens. I do not like being on my own, alone, undefined, forced to choose whatever I will. I feel a terrible nausea for life welling up in me. I would like to escape by default, to choose not to choose, but then this becomes a choice, and I meet myself face to face, filled with angst and despair.

My Primal and My Subsequent Choices. Out of my angst and nausea with life I must make a primal choice. I must choose to live or to die. Since for the moment I decide to live, I will live my life in such a way as to deserve something better than nothingness. I will use my becoming so as to deny the futility of existence and try to make my life a statement that ought never to be obliterated, even though I know that in the end it will be. Since essence is up to me, perhaps I can be worthy of existing and undeserving of being lost to the universe. I will try to have the courage to be. I will try to use my encounter with nothingness to affirm myself. I will try to have the courage to demonstrate my worth to a world in which my existence is not in question. I know that I exist, but I am aware that my *essence* is in question, and I want my essence to be worthy of existing forever.

Implications

Group members as well as the leader are faced with the task of defining their essence. This concept is fundamental to the existential view of the nature of man. A group cannot define essence for its members, who all share the human state of being thrown from oblivion into an ambiguous world. It does not follow, however, that interaction is an empty ritual. At first glance, this would appear to be the case, for if each person must be defined individually, what possible use could be made of group processes? If defining essence is an individual task, what place is there for the group relationship?

The answer lies in our essential loneliness. We are all alone but unaware of our essential state of isolation. If someone were dropped newborn on an unpopulated isle and by some miracle survived physically, that person would not become human in the existentialist sense. Individuals cannot define themselves without coming into contact with other humans. Only by interacting with others can we become aware that they exist. Only through this interface can a person define the self.

Groups provide a rare and valuable opportunity to experience ourselves through interacting with trained leaders and other members. Our need to define essence begs for opportunities to work with others, and a group experience can provide an unparalleled arena for this purpose. The essential, human lifelong task of defining essence is the most important process in which we are involved. A group is one place in which this can take place, as is shown in this dialogue on human loneliness being shared in a group setting.

> *Joan:* I feel uneasy when I walk into a room full of people. I don't know what to do, or say, or really, to be.
>
> *Jessica:* Yeah, that's how I am. I get tight inside, kind of queasy and don't know what to do.
>
> *Joan:* Right now I'm experiencing the same feelings. Kind of tight and sort of separate from you, and yet knowing you are here makes me feel stronger.

The Essence of the Group Leader

A group experience cannot change each member's essential need to define the self, but it can facilitate the process of becoming. Group members and leaders can walk together as each struggles with their essence. The group can share the pain of the constant transformation taking place, and by sharing can be energizers of the process. This sharing, however, holds special implications for the essence of leaders. If leaders are destructive, inauthentic, or unskilled, a member can be hurt.

Since a leader, as well as the member, is in the process of becoming, leaders require some source of human nourishment. One source of human nourishment for the leader is to participate in an ongoing group experience. Leading a group is stimulating but demanding. Group leaders may unconsciously find themselves using the groups they lead for their own needs, to the detriment of the group members. Therefore, maintenance groups for leaders seem essential as a way of professional life. It is a forum through which leaders can participate as members to maintain personal growth toward self-actualization.

Making Choices in an Extensional Group

The concept "existence precedes essence," with its reference to freedom, leaves us living an unanswered question. We must make choices and live by these choices. Since we must choose, our best chance of being human is to make as many choices as possible. The existentialist struggles constantly to maintain this awareness of freedom by trying to view every word and every act as an active choice so that values can be altered or revised as necessary.

One of the extensional group leader's tasks is to help members become aware of their own freedom. Freedom involves making choices. Participants can clarify the alternatives open to them and can increase their sensitivity toward making choices. The group leader helps members think through contradictions, ambiguities, value goals, and fantasies that may be action-inhibiting and may have blocked personal growth.

The consequences of alternatives can also be examined as members may be assisted to think through to logical conclusion various plans of action and, in so doing, develop awareness of personal freedom. Members also can examine the responsibility they carry for their chosen alternatives and face fully that they have no one on whom to shift this responsibility—neither counselor nor friend, teacher nor parent. They must also recognize that others will be affected by their actions and choices and as part of their individual responsibility be aware of the effect of their choices on others. Clarification of alternatives might be talked about in a group like this.

> *Jim:* I can't get a job unless I cut my hair, but I think it looks creepy short.
>
> *Jane:* You must not need a job very bad then.
>
> *Leader:* At the moment, you seem to be pulled two ways.
>
> *Jim:* I really am. I do need the job.
>
> *Sue:* You could buy a wig and push you hair up under it when you go look for a job.
>
> *Jim:* If I don't have a job, I don't have any money to buy a wig, do I? Besides, I'd feel stupid in a wig. I suppose I could cut my hair some.
>
> *Leader:* Of the ideas you have, having your hair at least somewhat shorter seems one alternative to consider.

Note that the leader adroitly avoids Sue's innocuous comment and gives Jim a way to respond as well as make a choice.

A group might talk about the responsibility for choice in this manner.

> *Harry:* I'm a listener. I want to be sure of what I say before I talk.
>
> *Al:* I think you are taking a free ride Harry. You take from the group, but you don't give anything back. I want to hear from you.
>
> *Leader:* Harry, I relate to your choosing to talk on your own terms. I also relate to your reaction, Al. I see you, Harry, as not being willing to carry your share of group responsibility. Do I have that right?

Humankind Is Condemned to Freedom

The Existentialist Paradox. I am free. No matter how much I would like to deny this fact, I cannot. I am free—and this freedom contains a paradox. Because of my freedom, the pronoun "I" has absolute priority in my existence. I am the only one of my kind, and I cannot be classified. Since I am a singular phenomenon, I never will be repeated. I ought to be worthy of attention in the world. I can understand Morris's (1966) comment, "I am permanent, a datum written with indelible ink into the cosmic ledger book, never to be erased or expunged. I may be in very small print, but I am there forever. I assign to myself, therefore...an absolute value and an ultimate worth" (p. 16). Because I exist and I am I, the world would not be quite the same without me. This is one side of the existentialist paradox.

The other side of the paradox that I hold in awareness is that my existence is a great delusion, a huge joke, because, as I think of the magnitude of the universe, I know that I count for absolutely nothing. The universe is indifferent to my presence. When I die, there may be a moment of stirring, but then nothing. Sooner than later my absence will be forgotten, and eventually all traces of me will be erased from the universe. I try not to think of this inevitability too much because it brings on nausea and angst, but always I am haunted by awareness that my existence is completely irrelevant.

This is the paradox with which I live: to matter and not to matter, to be of absolute value in the world and to be of absolutely no value. These two truths are contradictory, but both are true. My subjectivity asserts the absoluteness of my value, and my reason asserts the veracity of my valuelessness. These two facts are paradoxical, but I believe them both as an inescapable result of my being condemned to freedom.

My Absolute Freedom: I Am My Values. The thought of my absolute freedom makes me angry. I do not wish to be free, to choose for myself, to be condemned to making choices on my own. Surely there is someone or something who will direct me and eliminate the boundlessness of my responsibility. As it is, I must stand witness for all my statements as to who I am. I have total personal answerability for my involvement in life.

It is dread indeed to be free and aware of my freedom. The

responsibility for all my choices carries an added burden. As I make my choices, I create my value system. There is no one I can scapegoat, or blame, or burden with guilt. I would prefer an easier life, but I am free and am aware of my freedom. I am the sole author of my life, and I must answer for all I do. The statement that I make about myself is that I am ready to respond to each moment with authentic responsibility and am ready to speak for my performance.

This authenticity toward which I strive is elusive. I try to be honest inwardly and outwardly, but I am subject to error. At any given moment of being, I seem to myself to be authentic, but in backward glances I often find that my thoughts and behaviors were inconsistent with what I was really experiencing. I find that I cannot be wholly authentic, and this failure is a source of angst in me. I suffer pain because of anxiety and guilt generated by these failures. Intellectually I know that these failures are inevitable and a part of my human condition, but emotionally I react with a sense of incompleteness, a sense of never being total, a sense of freedom that is a burden rather than an inspiration.

In rare moments I transcend this sense of failure. At these times I am aware of moving forward, and I have a feeling of power over myself. In these instances I belong completely to myself and am in complete harmony with myself. I have the courage to be in full awareness, and I expect that in these moments I am truly authentic. At other times I can only use my sentence of freedom to strive toward authenticity and bear with what courage I can the angst that comes from failure. This is the inevitable tax levied with freedom, a price tagged to my condemnation.

Implications

The paradoxical nature of our freedom—to be of ultimate, absolute value and to be of absolutely no value—finds us in a condition of angst and nausea. We bring this angst and nausea to groups. The extensional group offers an antidote—human nourishment.

The concept of human nourishment applies especially to the extensional group. The notion, that just as we need adequate physical nourishment daily to sustain good somatic health, so do we require daily human nourishment to sustain good psychological health, is particularly relevant to the idea of group as a vehicle for optimum personality development.

In a regressive therapy group the concept of the group process functioning as a purgative, or cathartic, would be an apt parallel to the concept of human nourishment in an extensional group. A therapy group would eventually begin to supply the basic minimum requirements of psychological food to its members until they would be able to develop to the point at which they could obtain it from their life-spaces outside the group. The extensional group provides this automatically as members seek to extend themselves in self-actualization. Human nourishment and affirmation are spinoffs of the extensional group. The leader can help members recognize these basic needs that may be sought actively in life outside the groups. In an extensional group the human nourishment available should be abundant, and no one should leave the group psychologically hungry. In the following example not only is affirmation indicated among the group members but the concept of "universality" (Yalom, 1995) is noted—members experience sharing of the same feelings, "I am not alone in my experience."

> *Don:* I come to school in the morning, and I just go to class day after day, and I don't have any friends, and I wonder what's wrong with me.
>
> *Jim:* I know what you mean. The only time I get to talk with anyone is lunch time or on the phone at night.
>
> *Pete:* I'm glad to know you both feel the way I do. I thought I was the only one who didn't seem to have friends and who was alone all the time.
>
> *Leader:* It seems to me that each of you is saying that you

are lonely and that you also feel better knowing that someone is in the same boat—that there are others who feel the same way you do.

Existential Freedom and the Question of Values

The extensional group leader conceptualizes humankind as condemned to a freedom from which there is no escape. But the degree of awareness of that freedom differentiates existentialists from nonexistentialists. The former, having become aware of the implications of their freedom, must stand up to it as best they can. The nonexistentialist can enjoy the security of being other-directed.

At first glance the concept of freedom seems to pose problems for the extensional group leader, because the question of values is involved. Do leaders have the right to impose their values on a member?

Existentialism deals with this concern rather easily, for in this theoretical framework the question is irrelevant. Not only do leaders have no right to impose their values, but they *cannot* impose them, because we are all condemned to our own freedoms and must determine our own values. To raise the question of forcibly or subtly imposed values is to contradict the existentialist's concept of humankind as condemned to a freedom from which no escape is possible. This condition holds whether or not individuals are aware of their freedom; group leaders are condemned to freedom just as group members are.

The preceding notion in no way implies that leaders are not their value system. They are, and their values are transmitted full-force through their behaviors, but they do not impose these values on others. As leaders are available to members, so are their value systems available. Without this congruency, leaders could not be authentic. Leaders of extensional groups transmit to groups their feelings, their reactions, their essence. They are always aware, however, that their function as leaders is to assist the growth of group members, not to use the group for the leaders' own needs. As leaders of extensional groups interact with members, they are acutely aware that their sharing of authentic self is for the use of the group. Leaders are known, they are available, they are transparent, but they do not give advice or manipulate members. When they react and interact, they do so to extend the life-space of members. The fact that the leader's own life-space is expanded in the process is secondary to the primary purpose of being there—to be of use to the group. Here is an example of dialogue that reflects translation of this concept into action.

> *Member:* I wish I could be honest with people, but they wouldn't understand if I told them the truth.
>
> *Leader:* I feel closed out without a chance to know if I *could* understand.

In this dialogue the leader is stating clearly existent reactions—not needs (which might be to contradict or be "better than") but to make the essence available to the member, who can use this content to hear what is really being said: "I'm afraid I'll be rejected if I'm authentic; I prefer deceit," and so on.

Self Is Defined Only Through Actions

I am condemned by my human state to make free choices, and I know no reprieve from responsibility for those choices. On each choice I stake my future, and I am in a perpetual situation of crisis because I never am sure of the correctness of my choices. I also know that the way I define my essence is through my acts. I am continually emergent in my actions.

"What," Not "Why." I wish I could verbalize good intentions and get credit on the "books." I wish I could get credit for planning behavior and have it count, even though I didn't translate those plans into action. But I know that my plans, my good intentions, my regrets, my *whys* are irrelevant until translated into action. Verbalizing a commitment to change is not action.

What I actually do is my essence, my self-definition. Kierkegaard (1944) taught me this: that truth exists for a particular individual only as he or she produces it in action.

Thus, I must act before I count.

The "Here-and-Now." I do not restrict my conceptualization of action to overt acts but conceive my attitudes as part of the fabric of my actions. If I perform an act with reluctance, my reluctance defines some of that act. Everything that makes up my "I-ness" is relevant to my actions. The important idea of "I" is what I am *en toto,* and what I am now, this moment, here—not what I intend to be tomorrow, or what I intend to do tomorrow, or what I was yesterday, or what I did yesterday. This means that I must stand in present tense with complete accountability for what I am today, concerned about my past actions only as they are relevant for the present, and concerned about my future actions only as they are relevant for the present.

Implications

"Why" versus "What" Counseling. Extensional group leaders who subscribe to the defining-through-action concept do not ask "Why?" of a group member; this is considered irrelevant. Rather, focus of group exploration is on "What." For example, a member coming to the group with a conflict situation would not be faced with a futile cross-examination as to the causes of a behavior but would report the *what* of the circumstances. What were the behaviors, and what does the member see as alternatives to this action? And since the members are in charge of themselves and their actions, obviously any suggestion for solutions that requires a change of behavior by another person (e.g., a leader) would not be consistent with the concept that members are responsible for defining themselves.

In a school extensional group, for instance, emphasis on the *what* behavior of a member permits the existentialist leader to avoid the pitfall of defending a colleague. Since focus is on the actions of the participant, little attention is given to the actions of a teacher or other persons concerned. The insistence of the existentialist counselor that the counselees talk about their behaviors only may at first be annoying, but as the counselees grow in self-respect and self-acceptance, the increasing awareness of responsibility will be refreshing.

The emphasis on *what* counseling, which is consistent with the concept of defining the self through action, is productive to counselees and counselors alike. Here is an example of "what" dialogue.

> *Mary:* I try and try to be on time, but somehow I'm always late.
>
> *Leader:* It seems to me that the thing you *do* is be late. The thing you *intend* to do is be on time.

The Here-and-Now. The existentialist concept of existence being in the here-and-now implies that content is to focus mainly on the here-and-now process within the group. The fluid relating of one member to another provides the material of group exploration. As members react to each other, they are encouraged to verbalize this reaction. The current experiencing of each group member becomes the subject matter of each session. Concerns that each brings to the group are dealt with, of course, but the leader emphasizes existent reactions to those concerns and responds to the feelings of each member regarding the situation, rather than responding to the situation itself. Here is some group dialogue in the here-and-now.

> *Diane:* I'm really upset about what Joe did. He's mean and won't listen at all. He's impossible!
>
> *Leader:* I'm receiving a lot of anger and frustration from you right now. I guess your statement about you is that you're pretty angry with Joe.

Each existent moment in group represents an existential moment when a member and a leader decide to define their essence with courage or decide passively to resign their humanity. The courage *to be* requires that one live in continuous confrontation in and out of the group with one's being-in-the-world. A commitment to a decision-quality of human existence can be verbalized in the group. Living that commitment involves action outside the group.

Commitment stands on the statement: "This I am; this I believe; this I do. I am the being, the believing, the doing." Commitment is not a subscription to something external to one's life but an awareness, an attitude, and a recognition of the feeling of being fully present in a moment, making choices in that moment, and standing on the consequences of those choices. Participation in life and in the group is a consequence of genuine commitment to living in which one freely chooses one's being in action. If individuals take responsibility for their lives and express it through participation, they are totally involved, totally committed (Bugenthal, 1965). A participant can practice participative behavior in group life and perhaps increase involvement and commitment in life outside the group. The extensional group is an arena in which commitments can be articulated and extended into a member's entire life-space.

The "I-Thou" Relationship Defines Group Processes and Content

When I think of the "I-Thou" relationship, I become uneasy at times. What I must do to create this relationship is to communicate somehow my essence—open, uncensored, vulnerable. I do not always want to do this, partly because it will be, as it must be, only a shadow of my "I-ness," and also because in reaching I-to-thou I am risking the pain of being misunderstood or unaccepted. I would rather be safe in my obscurity. I would like to hide behind an anonymous mask; then no other could encounter the "I" of me, nor I, the "Thou" of the other. Thus, we never meet—and hurt. But also, we never meet—and love.

Journey into Life-Space. So I seek out the encounter "I-to-Thou," for here is where I exercise my being. In the encounter we live each other, reciprocating uniqueness and singularity. I enter the arena of another's life-space, vulnerable to all that is there. I am not neutral but am involved and committed. I risk pain and error, but I do this in awareness that encounter confirms my humanness, my authenticity, and my essence, just as it confirms the humanity, authenticity, and essence of Thou—all humankind. As I comprehend the essence of another, I take him or her into myself and allow myself to be taken into him or her, throwing open the gates of my being. We both experience an increasing inner richness.

This journey into the life-space of Thou is not easy for me. I must lower my defenses, allow my shields to go down, and, in a curious fashion, turn myself off, partially losing awareness of myself as a being with needs, drives, and perceptions as I try to enter the awareness of another. I do not know exactly how I do this, except that the act, I know, requires deep concentration, intense involvement, and maximum energy on my part.

In and out of encounter, I strive for perfect authenticity, but never am I complete, so I never outwardly transmit exactly what I am inwardly. I am never wholly congruent, but I struggle constantly toward becoming, always in the process of self-actualizing, never self-actualized. This imperfection becomes a source of angst, of anxiety, to me. I would like to be completed, but I cannot attain total authenticity, which I know is as unattainable as total encounter.

Implications

In the I-Thou relationship, the group leader enters a member's life-space and shares what is seen there. In openness and mutuality the existentialist leader allows the worlds of the participants to unfold during an encounter. This requires that the leader actively attempt to enter the members' worlds—not simply listen to them passively. The climate of the group is generated from empathy, congruency, and specificity on the leader's part. Members are helped to experience existence as real, to increase their abilities to extend potentialities and expand alternatives. Group members are assisted through the group process to ascend to their own statement of essence.

The extensional leader views members of the group as unique, dynamic individuals, not as statistical norms. Each member is not an object to whom things are done but a subject with whom action possibilities are explored. Each participant is treated with dignity as a person, whether child, adolescent, or adult. The leader encounters the person, regardless of age, as a being of ultimate value—a person who, like the leader, is engaged in defining essence out of ambiguous freedom.

Journey into Life-Space. Lewin's (1935) conceptualization of each individual existing in a life-space with parameters defined by the boundary that exists between self and the environment has application to the group process and relevance to the existential concept of encounter. A person's life-space is dynamically a relatively closed system that attempts to maintain equilibrium under the impact of field forces, negative and positive valences. The various life-spheres (profession, family, friendships) as well as different needs become more and more differentiated as individuals expand their life-spaces and extend psychical regions and systems within that life-space.

Encounter involves explorations of an individual's life-space. As some group members describe the territory of their psychical sphere, other members and leaders "track" verbalizations and in the process help each other understand, appreciate, and identify the forces in their idiosyncratic fields. In a somewhat mystical sense, the experience of a group focusing on the life-space of one member illuminates that space with the group's energies. As group members journey into the life-spaces of others in the group, human nourishment is given and received; insight concerning the realities of each individual's life-space also is gained. Somehow, as group members and leaders "walk around"

in one another's existences, obscured blocks to growth are identified and may then be dealt with. Characteristic lifestyles can
be identified too. A dialogue of such a journey is used for illus-
tration.

> *Harriet:* I look around my world, and it's all colored blue,
> and the people in it have dim faces. They aren't
> sad, but they aren't happy either.
>
> *Leader:* The way you describe it, they don't have much form,
> just seem to be blurs.
>
> *Harriet:* Yeah, people really don't have much meaning for
> me. Sometimes I think I just use them to get out of
> them what I want but don't see a real person behind
> the faces.
>
> *Leader:* Like right now, for instance, you seem somehow
> cut off, kind of in the distance, not quite right here,
> and I'm wishing I could reach you.

In addition to illuminating the life-space of each individual
group member, the group process can be used to explore the
relationship of one member's life-space to another's. The group
leader functions actively during this experience. A leader's responsibility is to aid members to encounter one another, and to
do this the leader must keep channels of communication open.

The existential emphasis on being responsible for the self
and appreciating the importance of acting and being in the here-
and-now is comparable with gestalt counseling procedures and
techniques (Passons, 1975) and the here-and-now group approach
(Yalom, 1995). Chapters 5 and 6, on leader functions, discuss
several techniques and group procedures taken from these approaches.

Summary

In this chapter we have identified concepts of existentialism relevant to the extensional group. The philosophy is presented from

a personal point of view, then translated into implications for the extensional group process. Illustrative dialogues have been provided.

3

Patterns of Interaction: Individual Behavior in the Group

Fundamental Interpersonal Relationship Orientation (FIRO)

From whatever perspective we chose to look at human behavior, the extensional group leader will begin to recognize that each human being is a unique combination of experiences, expectation, capabilities, values, motives, and belief systems. An appreciation for this uniqueness is easiest to encompass when talking about individuals rather than when dealing with members as a group leader. Observing human beings in action can be baffling, especially when trying to comprehend the interpersonal dynamics between group participants. Why do some group members hold back while others are almost compulsive about getting to know everyone? How is it that some people simply ooze warmth and caring while others recoil at the possibility of being touched? Why do some group members continually argue with the group leader and others seemingly refuse to take any form of responsibility for the group? Having a conceptual framework for organizing and making sense of what is happening between group members can be helpful in a group leader's decision making about how to proceed. Furthermore, when we begin to witness the many patterns of interaction, appreciation of human uniqueness acquires substance and practical meaning.

Schutz (1967) suggested that individuals can take care of three basic interpersonal needs—inclusion, control, and affection—through groups. Each of these three interpersonal needs, which can be viewed in terms of the way we express our needs to others and the way we want others to meet our needs, are described in detail.

Inclusion

When entering a room of relative strangers, some individuals immediately begin saying "hello," start conversations, and appear totally comfortable initiating the process of getting acquainted with others in the gathering. Other individuals do not initiate contact, preferring to sit back and wait for others to approach them. Some of those who do nothing to initiate contact with others welcome the overtures of others. Others do not care one way or the other whether people notice them or attempt to include them.

We all have varying needs for inclusion, the extent to which we want to be noticed by others. Some people have low inclusion needs; they simply do not need to be noticed. Some people may have a high need to initiate interpersonal contact but not be concerned about how this need is received by others. Others, who do nothing to initiate interpersonal contact, may desperately hope to be invited to be involved. The two aspects of inclusion are usually relatively balanced—that is, gregarious people usually hope for a receptive audience, and people who tend to hold back from making contact are likely to be selective about which outsiders and how many of them are permitted into their private worlds.

Group leaders can use Schutz's idea of inclusion needs to appreciate that quiet group members are not necessarily resistive. Leaders who understand the idea of inclusion and have a hunch about members' inclusion needs can begin to adapt their efforts with a sensitivity to each member's unique need for inclusion.

Control

Schutz makes an interesting comparison between inclusion needs and control needs. Inclusion, he has written, is a matter of predominance, whereas control is a matter of dominance. A person who has a high need for interpersonal control likes being in charge, making decisions for and about others, and being a significant influence in what happens. A person with a low need for interpersonal control prefers that others be responsible for themselves. We also must consider the degree to which we like others to control us. A highly dependent person needs to have others making decisions and, conversely, an independent person resists being controlled. In arguments or differences of opinion high controllers want to *win,* and they resist perceived authority. Low controllers generally have a "live and let live" attitude. They are not even particularly concerned about the issue of control. It is possible for one person to have almost opposite control needs; for example, an army sergeant may enjoy barking orders at recruits (high need to control others) and eagerly comply with orders from the commander (high need to *be* controlled by others). For the most part, however, there is usually an inverse correlation in control needs; the person who wants to be the boss normally does not like to take orders from others.

Group participants who are high controllers do not necessarily mean "trouble" for a group leader. Low controllers can cause more concern to a leader because of their unwillingness to be responsible or take a stand. It is important that group leaders be aware that apparently resistive or belligerent group members (high controllers) are displaying only a part of their interpersonal needs. Likewise, group members who are dependent, wanting others to decide and take responsibility, are revealing only a part of their interpersonal needs.

Affection

The third interpersonal need area is *affection,* which is loosely defined as warmth and caring. It characterizes the way individuals feel toward others and the way they want others to feel toward them. Schutz, in defining affection, includes a wide range of positive feelings. We can have a good feeling about someone we have just met, and we can have passionate feelings about an intimate. The focus is the extent to which we express our feelings toward others. Are we generous in hugging, stroking (verbally and physically), and expressing our positive feelings for others? Moreover, consider our degree of willingness to have others express their feelings toward us. A person who has low affection needs is not necessarily unfeeling. That person simply may not have the same needs as a person who wants affection from others and enjoys expressing it as well.

Some people assert their affectionate feelings, while others deal with these feelings in an entirely different manner. For some it is easier to initiate expressions of affection than to receive expressions of affection. Others are reluctant to display affection but are delighted to have others display affection toward them. And some individuals truly care nothing about affection displays.

Conclusion

As a group leader develops sophistication, it becomes possible to observe the group's interaction move through the three interpersonal need areas. In the opening session, if the members are strangers, inclusion needs prevail. The participants are wondering, "Who are these people, and how will I relate to them?" "Do I want to become involved with these people?" Once the inclusion issue is resolved, individual members begin jockeying for power in the form of wanting to be perceived as competent and influential. "Which group members seem to be the wisest, most compassionate, and alert?" "Which members are the better/best participants?" "Is anyone taking the leader to task?"

Bidding for power, influence, and dominance can be subtle, but it will be present. It has been said that if, for some reason, a group of strangers were to be assembled, a leader would naturally emerge. Leadership is a form of control (power), and leaders must be aware of their own styles of leadership, as well as being sensitive to the control needs of group participants.

After the inclusion and control needs are clarified, affection is the next stage of group development in an extensional group. Openness, trust, and warmth are shared by group members who have consciously (or unconsciously) come to terms with their inclusion and control needs. They are comfortable with their identity in the group and have assessed the potential importance of their contribution to the group.

Although the complexity of the various interpersonal patterns can be overwhelming, awareness of the three interpersonal needs provides a basic conceptual framework for organizing experience and observation. Adroitness at altering strategies and techniques is an art rather than a skill, but the leader needs a beginning framework nonetheless. Being aware of the three interpersonal needs is a foundation. Group members do indeed vary in their uniqueness. They have their own needs and their own contribution to make to the group. The FIRO (Schutz, 1977) is one way of organizing the interactive need of group participants.

The Johari Window

The Johari Window (Luft, 1963) offers the group leader and members a framework that provides direction for the group processes. The model demonstrates what happens in member interactions within the group process. Figure 3.1, an adaptation of the conceptual scheme of Luft, illustrates how appropriate disclosure develops as the process occurs. A description of what the four quadrants represent in the group process follows.

Quadrant I: Known to Self; Known to Others
(Area of Free Activity)

The first quadrant of the Window represents content that is known to me about me and is readily available or is known to others. This content is the fabric of social intercourse around which

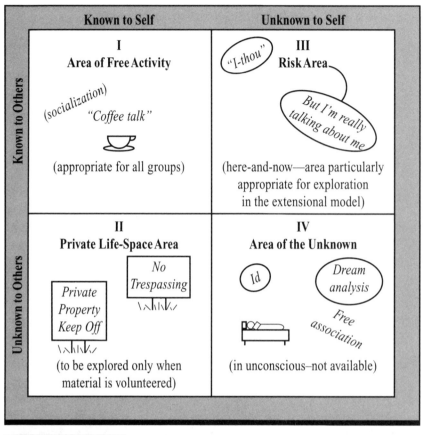

FIGURE 3.1

A Cognitive Map of Group Processes (Adapted for Groups from the Johari Window)

Source: *Group Processes: An Introduction to Group Dynamics* by Joseph Luft. Reprinted by permission of Mayfield Publishing Company, copyright 1984, 1970, and 1963 by Joseph Luft.

we build our daily interchanges. Out of this knowledge, known to me and known to others, can be built a commonality of interest that may lead to friendship. We routinely use this content area in social situations to build and to perpetuate relationships.

We operate in this quadrant in our daily interactions and with one another. As we expand the size of the quadrant, we come to know more about each other and may come to care more for each other. The content material of this quadrant is primarily cognitive, although it may contain some conative content. The prime characteristic is that this content is typical of material we deal with in routine activities. Therefore, although it's useful as a vehicle from which to build group communication and group acquaintanceship, interaction in this quadrant is not unique to groups but may be obtained in a variety of circumstances.

Quadrant II: Known to Self; Unknown to Others (Private Life-Space)

This quadrant represents the body of knowledge each of us knows about ourselves but which is not shared with others. This knowledge concerns our private, personal lives. If, in a group, members or leaders intrude into that private, personal area, they have trespassed into another's life-space. No one in a group is welcomed to solicit material from this quadrant. When members volunteer content from their private, personal life-space, it is available to the group. Until that time, the "No Trespassing" sign must be observed.

A group member may choose to bring concerns from Quadrant II of his or her life-space to the group where they can be discussed. However, the material must directly concern that person and not others close to him or her. Participants in interaction groups sometimes inappropriately introduce material that concerns Quadrant II life-space of significant others in their lives. Consider, for example, a member who relates that his wife is a sloppy housekeeper and cannot manage their money. The group leader suggests that the group member deal with *his* feelings about the situation, not his wife's behaviors. Thus, the focus is maintained on the existent experience in the here-and-now of the group member, not on the past or present experience in the

there-and-then—in this instance, a wife's housekeeping behaviors.

Leaders do not allow members to probe into private areas
of each others' lives. They do not allow one member to volunteer another member's material, nor do leader's do so themselves.

In regard to Quadrant II material, the issue of confidentiality usually arises. In most groups, members are requested to
keep confidential all material derived from this quadrant. When
students are involved, material from this quadrant must be handled
with particular care because the school group leader is rarely
able to guarantee confidentiality on behalf of student group
members. A recourse would be to discourage exploration of
material from this quadrant that would violate the privacy of a
member's family. For example, if a student wishes to discuss a
family argument, the leader should move away from a detailed
description of the event and assist the member in dealing with
here-and-now feelings and behaviors in relation to the event.

Quadrant III: Unknown to Self; Known to Others (The Risk Area—The Group Arena)

If a leader takes the position that Quadrant I is useful—but not
unique—to groups and is available in a variety of settings, that
Quadrant IV is by definition not available, that Quadrant II in-
vades privacy and may be volunteered only if it concerns the
member, what areas can be tapped so that the group process is
productive? The answer lies in Quadrant III. Here can be found
material unique to groups and, in usual human interface, not
tapped.

There is a body of material that is *known to you about me*
but that I do not know about me; that is *known to me about you*
but that you do not know about you. This risk area concerns the
way I am experiencing you and the way you are experiencing
me. You, and *only* you, are the sole source of information about
how you are reacting to me, and I have no way of obtaining
these data until you are willing to give them to me. Conversely,

I and *only* I, am the sole source of information about how I am reacting to you, and you have no way of obtaining these data until I give them to you.

If the uniqueness of the group process is to be tapped, I must be willing to give you feedback out of this risk area. As I communicate with you concerning my response to you, it must be understood that there will be no implication that you should change. You may or may not choose to do so. If a number of group members experience the same reaction, you may give the feedback more weight. However, you may choose only to recognize their statements as useful information to be "filed."

Quadrant III taps solely the *here-and-now* of the group process—how one member is experiencing another in that existent moment. Content does not deal with life outside the group but with what is going on within the group. Members can use the group process as an arena in which honest, genuine, uncensored feedback is given "I to Thou." Negative reactions may be expressed, but just as many, if not more, positive reactions will probably be expressed. The interaction takes place at a level of intense experiencing together of each passing moment, and the experiencing is described verbally.

Such interactions are appropriate in only a few situations outside a group. If, in routine social intercourse, people were to describe their ongoing reactions to each other at this level of intensity, economic productivity would probably be diminished. Frequent bulletins from "viscera land" become ludicrous, and, unless all concerned are operating from Quadrant III agendas, the misunderstandings that could occur would be countless and disastrous. Such discussions "in group" are another matter.

The interaction group is unique in that it is the total agenda for each member to obtain honest feedback on how others are experiencing them. This requires that members of a group risk themselves to perform this "act of grace." When members respond to each other out of Quadrant III, they are giving a part of themselves not usually offered. They are risking rejection and misunderstanding. By lowering their defenses, they become open and vulnerable. Feedback of this kind represents a gift of great value—an act of grace, something of infinite worth, a part of another human being.

This act of grace—giving authentic feedback and receiving the gift of honest reaction—is built on a principle that must be transmitted to the group by the leader and then reinforced through-out the life of the group. This principle is basic to this area of communication: "When I speak, I speak only about me, about my values, about what I feel is good or bad for me. My feed-back to you is a statement about me. If I react to you in an as-sertive or attacking manner, or if I relate to you in a neutral or nonrisking monologue, or if I relate to you in a caring, empathic way, I am communicating how it is with me, and I am risking something of my essence."

Long before the extensional group existed, Buddha recog-nized this truth: that when a person speaks, he or she speaks only of and for himself or herself. A parable tells the story of a foolish man who, learning that Buddha observed the principle of returning good for evil, came and abused him. Buddha was silent until the man finished. Then he asked him, "If I decline to accept a gift made to me, to whom then does the gift be-long?" The man answered, "In that case, it would still belong to the person who offered it." Buddha replied, "Since I decline to accept your abuse, does it not then belong to you?" The man made no reply but walked slowly away, carrying with him that which he had wished to give to another (Siu, 1968).

Quadrant IV: Unknown to Self; Unknown to Others (Area of the Unknown)

Quadrant IV represents material that by definition is unavail-able—the unconscious. It does, however, represent the potential for growth. Working through the first three quadrants, material originally unknown to an individual may come forth. Gener-ally, in extensional groups leaders do not seek to bring the un-conscious into awareness. In fact, for the leader to deal with materials in Quadrant IV requires a high degree of skill and training, thus, the quadrant is "off limits" for extensional groups.

Summary

Two conceptual frameworks for comprehending interaction among group members have been presented: FIRO and Johari Window. Each of these concepts views interpersonal contact from a different perspective. The FIRO framework stresses the interpersonal needs that differ on an individual basis. The Johari Window framework stresses interpersonal interaction that includes commonly known information between two persons as well as a degree of knowledge and awareness on the part of each that is independent and unknown to the other. When unknowns are shared (self-disclosure), the probability of trust and interpersonal effort increases. Each of the frameworks offered provide some degree of clarity and organization to the reader for consideration of these complexities.

4

Leader Techniques:
The Basics

Group norms are introduced in the initial phase of group leadership. They are subtle and ongoing in nature. There are no pronouncements of rules and regulations—no do's; no don'ts. Instead, effective facilitating techniques are necessary, which, according to Kottler (1994), require the utmost perseverance "to hold the client's attention over the long haul, to encourage creative solution seeking, to facilitate spontaneous, productive interaction, and to help clients take risks" (p. 116). Once the basics have been learned, the leaders must expand the base of fundamental helping skills necessary for survival as a group leader. By establishing group norms—which do not come by accident but only through diligence and a consistent leadership style—a "therapeutic system" necessary for personal growth is established (Yalom, 1995). A description of leader techniques as well as examples of appropriate leader interventions will be presented in this chapter.

Opening a Session

Leaders need to have some general leads at their command to use in opening sessions. These might be: "We can begin anywhere you like," "Let's get started," or "It's time to begin." These statements simply give the signal that the group is in session.

Group leaders also may want to use some of the confrontation techniques, both verbal and nonverbal (see Chapter 5), to begin a group, but there is a danger that the group will become dependent on the leader always to initiate interaction. If leaders allow this to happen, they are depriving members of the opportunity to develop independence and autonomy. Therefore, if leaders choose to use some interaction stimulators in one session, they should not take complete responsibility for initiating interaction in the next.

Leaders also may begin a group with silence, waiting for a member to initiate verbal communication. The danger in this is that the silence can become punitive. If it does, leaders have responsibility for breaking the silence. They might do so by sharing where *they* are and how *they* feel. Leaders have no more right to volunteer a member than one member has the right to volunteer another. The only legitimate tools leaders possess to model here-and-now behaviors are themselves (or the co-leaders). This is not to imply that leaders ever become members of their groups—they are *always* the leaders; they are there for the gain of the members. Leaders must join their own growth or maintenance groups if they wish to become members.

The "go-around" is helpful to open a session. The leader may suggest, for example, a go-around in which each member shares how he or she is feeling at that very minute. After making the original suggestion, the leader may continue to comment for a few seconds, having made clear where the go-around will begin and the direction it will take. The leader can initiate the experience by sharing of himself or herself, asking for feedback, thus modeling group membership behavior. Then the leader may encourage the others to participate. The reason for the delay between the suggestion and implementation is to give members a moment to prepare themselves, to marshal their thoughts—in other words, to avoid surprises that generate defensive reactions.

Beginning group leaders often make the mistake of assuming that a group will begin one session right where the last session ended. This is a faulty assumption. When a group parts, each member (and the leader) continues the internal dialogue with self for many hours. During these "self-conversations" growth takes place, insights occur, understandings develop.

Thus, it is naive to assume that a group will begin where it ended. Rather, leaders should assume that the group members are in quite a different place from where they were when they left off. Leaders should attempt to begin each session, then, in the here-and-now, making no assumptions about the there-and-then.

Communication

Attending Behavior

Group leaders may not be aware of some of their nonverbal messages, particularly those that transmit attending or nonattending behavior. The use of videotape recordings can help increase the leader's awareness of this kind of behavior.

Ivey, Normington, Miller, Morrill, and Hasse (1968) have used attending behavior as their initial focus in microcounseling—working with the one-to-one relationship—but their observations are relevant to the leader's work. Three focal points of attending behavior have been identified with both verbal and nonverbal components.

The first is *eye contact*. If leaders do not maintain eye contact with their members, members are likely to feel they are being treated as objects rather than subjects. A major vehicle for transmitting empathy is eye contact; thus, group leaders should be acutely aware of what they are doing with their eye "language."

A second component of attending behavior is *postural movement and gestures*. A group leader can transmit the message, "I hear, I understand, I feel," through body posture.

The third element, *verbal following behavior*, also transmits attending or nonattending. Beginning leaders have difficulty "tracking" accurately the outputs of a member in a one-to-one relationship, and it is infinitely more difficult to track accurately the outputs of members of a group. Nonetheless, this is what group leaders must do, and they must respond in a way that allows group members to know they are being heard. Leaders should respond easily in a variety of modes: reflection of content, reflection of feeling, clarification, and general leads. Nonverbal cues are discussed more thoroughly in Chapter 5.

Feedback

Giving and receiving feedback is the life stream of a group. Without it, the group has no reason for existing. Yet the leader cannot assume that members are sensitive to this kind of communication. Generally in our daily lives we receive little feedback, and almost never the honest kind that is the *sine qua non* of group life. Without feedback, we blindly continue making the same mistakes day after day. Even though we may be dimly aware that something is amiss in our behavior, we are seldom able to specify exactly which behaviors are causing our discomfort. We do not know just what we are doing that causes unwanted reactions in others. Consequently, we do not possess the raw materials of change—the awareness of unwanted behaviors.

It is no accident that we do not routinely give and receive feedback in our daily lives. Doing so is extremely difficult, and it involves a personal risk that most people are not willing to take. It also involves a commitment to another human being, which is indeed rare. And it requires a skill not commonly possessed.

If group members are to learn how to give and receive feedback, group leaders must transmit this information through modeling in their own behavior and, perhaps, through direct instruction.

Feedback is not always helpful. Leaders have to be alert to the motives behind members' feedback offerings. Often the material is rejecting rather than confrontive, and the primary motivation of the member who is giving the feedback is to punish another group member in some way or to make the giver of the feedback feel better. If such situations occur, the leader is responsible for calling attention to his or her own reaction to the feedback and questioning the member's motives. Also, members may engage in "groupie" behavior in the guise of feedback, using their verbalizations to demonstrate how sophisticated, perceptive, or brilliant they are.

Then again, feedback may be motivated by a caring for someone else and a willingness to share oneself, despite the risk this entails. Feedback must be specific to be helpful, and it must deal with behaviors that are current and that can be changed. For example, if one member comments to another, "I think you are very unfriendly," the leader might ask the commenting member to specify exactly what behaviors of this "unfriendly" member gave rise to such an impression. (And, as always, the leader emphasizes that in all our statements we are essentially talking about ourselves!)

Feedback should be verbalized so that it is clearly related to the frame of reference of the person offering the feedback. Thus, "I am getting tense sitting next to you because you have been tapping your foot for several minutes," would be preferable to, "You are tense tonight. What is the matter?" Early in a group's life the leader may have to intervene frequently to insist that speakers talk from their own point of view—where they are—rather than focus their comments on the member who is the target of the feedback. As members learn how to give self-centered feedback, the leader will have to intervene much less frequently.

Feedback must not be perceived as a mandate for change. Again and again the leader must emphasize that givers of feedback are describing how it is with them and that the receiver may do with the comments whatever he or she chooses. If receivers of feedback choose to change, it must be because they want to, not because a member of the group "suggests" that they do so. Every member should be helped to realize that no one has the right to ask another to change. Feedback only transmits information about how it is with the sender; it does not solicit changes on the part of the receiver.

A curious situation often occurs in the giving of "pseudo-feedback." One member might comment to another, "I used to find you cold and unfeeling, but now I find you warmer," and then wait expectantly for a response. The receiving person inevitably feels that a burden is placed on them and that they are expected to do something with it. In actuality, this person is left with nothing to say except an inane, "That's nice" or a rude, "So?" or an uncomfortable, "I like you too." The original comment was a subtle form of "groupie" behavior that is difficult for a leader to handle without seeming to reprimand. The leader could call attention to the comment's hook of when-did-you-stop-beating-your-wife, or intervene with a comment about how the pseudo-feedback made the leader feel. The giver of the pseudo-feedback probably had good intentions, but this kind of interaction is *not* authentic feedback—which must have a handle on it that will enable the receiver to deal with it and respond to it.

Using the same example, real feedback might have gone like this: "I feel bad that I used to see you as cold and uncaring and would like to ask for your understanding of my blind spot." In this case the receiver is left with a handle by which to respond, and the interaction can continue. (The behavior of difficult members is discussed further in Chapter 8.)

Group interaction is based on feedback. The effectiveness of a group depends on the quality of the feedback contained in the group's interaction, and the group leader is responsible for controlling the quality of that feedback. From honest, helpful feedback group members may gain self-understanding and an increased awareness of the effects of certain of their behaviors on others; they may become more sensitive to contradictions between their verbal and nonverbal messages; they may come to understand distortions in their communication patterns; they may experience a heightened sense of self as delightful, exciting, warm, and loving human beings. Here is an example of feedback dialogue.

> *Leslie:* I wish someone would help me understand how I'm coming on "child."
>
> *Don:* You sit in a little-girl way.
>
> *Leader:* Don, it would be helpful if you were more specific.
>
> *Don:* Well, Leslie, you fold your hands in your lap, and you tip your head to one side when you are coming on "child."

Confrontation

Confrontation offered with empathy is a gift. Confrontation offered with animosity is not a gift. The line that divides the two lies within the confronter. Caring, unconditional positive regard, congruency, authenticity, and *agape* (making no demand in return) render confrontation a gift of great value. Without these characteristics confrontation can become twisted by hostility and diminish both receiver and sender.

Anderson (1968) has found that if the leader operates with a high degree of empathy, with positive regard to the client, genuineness, concreteness, and self-disclosure, the offering of confrontation will be facilitating. However, if the leader operates at low levels of empathy, does not truly care for the client, and is inauthentic and fearful of risking, confrontation will be experienced by the client as criticizing, unfeeling, and overly intellectual. Leaders who consistently operate at a high level of interaction tend to respond to the strength and resources of a group member, while leaders who function at a low level tend to respond to members' weaknesses.

The benchmark of confrontation is the risk leaders take with themselves in making the verbal response. They clearly state their position, feelings, and perceptions. They state them in the here-and-now; and they are discrepant with those offered by the member. For example, a member might say:

> I couldn't do my homework again last night because the teacher didn't make it clear, and I forgot to take my book home any-

way. Besides, there was too much noise in the house because my dad and mom were looking at TV.

A confrontation by the leader might be:

I'm feeling somewhat irritated by your comment. It seems you are blaming everyone else and that you never intended to do the work.

In this confrontation the member knows that the leader disagrees and that the leader is expressing real feelings (anger) of the moment. The member knows that the leader cared enough to risk in a way that could have caused rejection.

The purpose in confronting is to share perceptions and to communicate authentically—*not* to prove one's point. The leader must keep this purpose in mind when helping members confront each other. Confrontation is not intended to identify the "right" view or to establish one's superiority over another. Attackers are trying to win or to dominate. In confrontation, the information being offered could easily have been concealed rather than shared. Confrontation means providing another person with a different perspective from which to view a problem or revealing observed behavior of which another person is unaware. Confrontation is a caring act. It is also a form of feedback. What the recipient does with the feedback is entirely up to him or her.

Confronting a speaker who generalizes excessively is also helpful at times in maintaining group interaction. For instance, in a high school group a student had made the remark that no one in the whole world really cared what his thoughts and opinions were. Another student confronted the speaker with, "Hey man, wait a minute. You've included me as someone who doesn't care—and that simply ain't so. I care about you and what's important to you."

A leader who engages in confrontation is taking a risk and knows it. The confronter cannot always be certain how others will respond to the information being presented. A leader who confronts a member with his or her perception risks being misunderstood. The member may feel demeaned although the leader did not intend to do that. Often, members may put more stock in a leader's perception than in a fellow group member's because they perceive the leader's status as reinforcing. What the leader says may be interpreted as "fact," but stating "facts" is not the purpose of confrontation. The leader must model confronting behavior and must be prepared to review the subjective nature of confrontation as often as may be necessary to help the group.

Confrontation, then, represents a more intense and important form of feedback in that the speaker (the confronter) assumes responsibility for what is being shared. Our perceptions can be only tentative and subjective. Normally, perceptions change as additional information is provided and experience is gained. That is why confrontation in group interaction is so valuable. Group leaders or members who are willing to share their perceptions are offering information to which the receiver does not normally have access—someone's perception of him or her. We reiterate that what one does with the information, whether it alters one's attitude or behavior, is entirely up to the receiver. Confrontation is not offered to force change in the receiver. It is offered as a gift.

Confrontation differs from interpretation, because interpretation means that the leader is making an observation based on some theoretical postulate or inference. For example, if the leader had wished to interpret the member's comment about his homework, she might have said, "I think you are rationalizing all around the issue. You are giving *good* reasons, but not the real ones." Interpretation often focuses on the past (a search for explanations of behaviors in previous occurrences) whereas confrontation always focuses on the present moment. Both confrontation and interpretation, however, consist of content to which members can react emotionally and thus, perhaps, gain insight into their own functioning.

Anderson (1968) stated that a confrontation can be said to have occurred if:

1. The client describes himself to the therapist in terms of what he wishes to be (his ego-ideal) rather than what he is (his real self), whereupon the therapist faces the client with his own experience of the situation.
2. The client expresses an increased awareness of himself (insight) as if this were the magical solution to all his problems; that is, there is a discrepancy between the client's insights and his actions in relation to these insights. (p. 411)

Confrontation is an act of kindness. In this process the confronter takes a risk, but in so doing sends a message to the receiver that he or she, the confronter, cares enough to take that risk and respects the integrity and self-determination of the receiver. The confronter is saying, "I respect you, I value you, and I believe you have the strength to receive me fully—uncensored and giving all of myself, my reactions, and my perceptions. Knowing that you may reject me, I am giving you some of my essence. I do this because I care for you." These two dialogues represent confrontation in group interaction.

Dick: I don't like you, Mary. You are a manipulating female, and you make me mad.

Mary: Dick, I experience you as using me to get rid of your hostilities toward women, and I don't like you to do that, because I want your acceptance and caring.

Ken: That dumb teacher picks on me all the time.

Edsel: Aw, Ken, you bring it on yourself, and because I care for you, I get mad when you make statements like that. You cause the trouble and you try to blame the teacher. I would like to help you if I can.

Closing a Session

Groups must begin and end on time. Through groups, members test and learn limits, and if leaders exceed the agreed-upon limits, they are abdicating their responsibility and reinforcing a perception many group members may already have—that people often don't mean what they say, that they cannot be trusted. The same rationale applies to the number of sessions. An eight-session group is just that—not an eight-plus-two group. Neophyte group leaders may have difficulty beginning and ending an individual group session on time and terminating the group itself, but, as they gain experience, they come to realize the importance of doing both.

Capping

To end at a previously agreed time, leaders need a technique to bring the group back to the nongroup world—the real, outside world. They do this through *capping*. Somewhere near the end of a session, leaders should begin to ease up interaction. Emotional content should be tapered off and cognitive processes made dominant. Leaders do this by responding deliberately to *ideas* and *generalities*, to cognitive rather than conative content. In this way the group is brought away from deep emotional exploration and toward preparation to function in their usual life-spaces in the world of social reality. The amount of time the leader requires for this process depends on the sophistication of the group, the destination of members when they leave the group (e.g., home, classroom, job, lunch), and the depths of interaction at which the group was working.

Leaders may not wish to cap every group, but they always have to make sure that no member is left in a state of crisis. No member should leave a group session unable to cope with his or her world. At the same time, leaders do not want to close the door on a member's growth, which (unfortunately) may involve some discomfort.

Summary

The role of the group leader has been discussed in this chapter, and the implications for the use of interventions in creating a group culture have been examined. The use of facilitation techniques such as confrontation, attending behavior, feedback, and misuse of questions as a technique were addressed. A discussion of procedures for opening and closing sessions and a section on capping also were included.

5

Developing
Good Group
Communication
Skills

The Role of the Leader

Creative leaders are role models and mentors; they are competent in the technical aspects of group leadership. Whether leaders are working with a psychotherapy group or an extensional group, they are required to be nourishing human beings; that is, they must offer warmth, encouragement, and reinforcement. The leader facilitates human growth and development. In the words of Kottler (1994), the leader is best described as "a wise adviser, a guide, a sponsor, a teacher...who encompasses the virtues of competence, wisdom, and ethics" (p. 87). In light of these marks of distinction, appropriate leader techniques are the cornerstone of effective leadership. Notwithstanding all considerations of technique, the relationship between leader and group member is supreme. Consistent and ever positive, the relationship embodies "concern, acceptance, genuineness, empathy. Nothing, no technical consideration, takes precedence over this attitude" (Yalom, 1995, p. 106).

Numerous authors have provided descriptions of leader qualities thought to be important (Corey, Corey, & Callanan, 1993; Friedman, 1989; Shapiro, 1978; Trotzer, 1989). Kottler (1994) describes good leadership as demonstrating the qualities of energy, knowledge, skill, and enthusiasm. Among the features that distinguish effective and productive group leaders from others, Kottler would include: "an affinity for an attraction to group environments; special cognitive styles such as the ability to process multiple stimuli simultaneously and sort through information to find the most significant focus; interpersonal attitudes similar to those of superlative teachers...and greater adaptability and flexibility to change direction fluently, depending on what is happening" (p. 90).

The role of extensional leaders is characterized by professional expertise coupled with clear acceptance of the responsibility of leadership. Leaders, in the final analysis, define the role. Who they are—their authenticity, awareness, degree of self-actualization, empathy, intelligence, self-acceptance, in short, their "humanness"—is the most relevant variable leaders bring to group leadership (Dreyfus, 1962). An understanding of the dimensions of group leadership is essential preparation for the developing leader.

Leader interventions interrelate; they complement and supplement one another. Group leadership is more than the sum of the components. It is a symbiotic relationship: a process of synthesizing and integrating intervention skills. In the beginning leaders help members become aware of behaviors that open communication channels or those that inhibit communication. As members learn the responsibility of group membership, leader interventions diminish. It is important, however, that leaders take an active role in the early sessions, remaining adroitly consistent in monitoring the response mode of the group members.

Opening Communication Channels

Staying in the Present Tense

Existing as a group member in the present time and place (here-and-now) is one of the most difficult tasks of group members. Even with constant interventions from the leader, it takes most group members three or four sessions before they are able to relate their comments and responses to the here-and-now of group life. Interventions by leaders can help refocus the group on the immediate experiencing of members and away from the past or rehearsals for the future. Although some there-and-then content may be appropriate, the leader should constantly monitor content for its current relevancy. What do members' verbalizations mean to them right now? What is the member saying to another member right now? A number of strategies can be used by group leaders to interrupt negative communication patterns.

Avoiding the "We"

As members talk about the there-and-then world, they tend to talk in generalities, using "we," "people," "all of us," and "they," rather than taking full responsibility for their comments by speaking in the first person. Appealing to the authority of the majority is a common way by which people control one another. A leader must intervene in the group so that members learn to accept responsibility for their own statements. The prelude to taking responsibility is to recognize first those habitual speech patterns that shift authority to others. The following dialogue illustrates Sue's attempts to generalize her feelings and the group leader's interventions to help Sue personalize her communication in the group.

> *Sue:* Last week, during group, I was really shook up at the apathy this group has toward people's problems.
>
> *Leader:* And apparently you still have feelings about it now.
>
> *Sue:* Yeah, as a group we haven't helped each other at all.
>
> *Leader:* It seems to me, Sue, that you can only talk for yourself. You may want to share your thoughts.
>
> Sue: Okay. I don't feel that I've been helped by anyone here at all, and I wish someone would help me.
>
> *Leader:* Would you be more specific, please? Maybe there is someone in particular that you have in mind...here...now.
>
> *Sue:* Yeah...you, John, and you, Mary, and you, Pete—I wish each of you would give me something about

what it is that might make people think I don't care about them. That's the message I've been getting from you three, and I'm disturbed by it. I guess I've also been saying that the *group* doesn't care...and I think that's what you've been telling me.

Leader: Understand, Sue—John, Mary, and Pete are individuals. They can only speak for themselves. *They* are not the *group*.

Pete: I would like to respond, Sue, and give you some feedback on how you have come across to me.

Avoiding Super-Mothering

"Super-mothering" is not restricted to the female sex. Males, as well as females, often intervene in confrontations in an effort to assuage hostility, guilt, and pain. This has also been referred to as "Band-Aiding." Although super-mothering is done in an apparent effort to be helpful, it is actually highly manipulative. Probably few members recognize their interventions as motivated by their own inability to confront these emotions, that doing something for someone always has an element of manipulation in the act.

Often in group, one member may be engaged in a confrontation with another member when another participant interjects a "soothing" comment. The intensity of the confrontation may be lessened and may even be diverted by the super-mothering behavior. Unfortunately, this loss of intensity may take away the opportunity for the member being confronted to face some intra- or interpersonal conflict that might be a source of growth. The leader should divert the super-mothering intervention so the confrontation may be completed to resolution. Here are two examples of this kind of leadership intervention.

John: Jim, when you shake your finger at me like that, I get all tight inside.

> *Mary*
> *(to John):* Jim doesn't mean anything by it. He's just making a point.
> *Leader:* Mary, it appears that you are denying John's feelings. John is saying something he wants Jim to hear.
>
> *Sarah:* I feel betrayed. I believed him, and now I know he lied to me. I guess I'm partly angry because I see myself as being taken advantage of and made a fool of.
> *Mary:* Well, Sarah, we all have felt that way at times. I think everybody is made a fool of at one time or another. I remember once when my friend...
> *Leader:* Excuse me, Mary. Sarah is talking about something that is important to her. You were saying, Sarah, that you are feeling angry and foolish about being deceived?

Forestalling Mind-Raping

Another difficult intervention to make is that of calling attention to the dynamic in which one participant makes assumptions about what another is thinking or feeling. Members who are thus "interpreted" are negated and illegitimatized. Their minds are raped, and they are likely unaware of the process. Leaders should make the group aware that such has occurred.

Mind-raping may be confused with feedback. The difference is subtle, but in feedback a participant is "reading" another's thoughts. When mind-raping occurs, the member providing the "feedback" is making unfounded assumptions about another's feelings.

Here are three examples of mind-raping. Notice that the group leader intervenes each time Henry's feedback becomes harmful.

> *Maria:* I wish I could like you, Henry, but I always have a feeling of wanting to get away when I'm with you.

Henry: That's because you think I'm judging you.

Leader: Henry, you're putting thoughts into Maria's mind and throwing the responsibility onto her.

Henry: Okay, Maria, I guess I can't speak for what is in your mind, but when I am with you this is how I feel.

Maria: When I am with you, Henry, I have a need to get away from you...I feel uneasy.

Henry: Yeah, you have uneasiness in the stomach, you have fears of being with me, you have unrecognized sexual responses, and you really would like to confront me, but you can't.

Leader: Henry, you have put words to feelings that you only assume Maria has. I'd rather hear how it is with Maria from Maria.

Maria: When I am with you, Henry, I feel...

Henry: Mm-hmm, uneasy, uptight, like you would not want to be there, anxious.

Leader: Henry, you interrupted Maria and have not allowed her to finish how it is with her.

Deterring Questions

The intervention that meets with the most resistance is blocking questions. Out-of-group speech patterns rely heavily on the questioning form of communication. The awareness that the questioner controls the responder in a subtle way is rarely perceived by most people. Within the group process, members tend to bring to the group a heavy reliance on questions as a way of communicating. As a result, the receiver can be intimidated. To prevent constant questioning, leaders must help group members recognize this traditional way of controlling communication. Members need to be encouraged to make a clear statement of what is meant. At first members may feel angry and hostile and manifest impatience and resistance. It is important for leaders to monitor the irritation of members and determine when intervention is likely to be inhibiting or facilitating, then use good judgment as to when to intervene and when to abstain. A leader must question gently, without rejecting the questioner. Here are two ways a group leader might accomplish this.

John: Why do you feel like that, Paul?

Leader: John, you have phrased your concern so that Paul doesn't know how it is with you. I feel it will be more helpful if you make it clear what you have in mind.

John: Paul, I guess I don't relate to what you're saying because I don't think I would feel that way.

Note that John's first statement implies judgment. His second statement is a clear message of where he stands concerning the issue, and where he stands with Paul.

Mary: Ralph, do you get mad when that happens?

Leader: Rather than ask Ralph a direct question, as the question may have more to do with you, I wonder if you could make it clear how you feel about it, Mary.

Mary: He makes me mad, Ralph. I want you to say how you feel about the situation, and I'm irritated with you because you haven't.

In this example the leader has helped Mary to "own" her feelings rather than work them out vicariously through Ralph.

Communicating Without Questions

When Leaders Ask Questions

As mentioned previously in this chapter, productive leadership requires controlling the process, not controlling the group members. The trap inherent in the use of questions as a leadership technique is that questions do control group members. The most efficient method of keeping members in submission is to inter- rogate them. In this way leaders can appear to be the "author- ity" who seeks information from others without revealing too much of themselves. They can exercise iron control over mem- bers by firing questions at them, particularly "why" questions (Passons, 1975). If the leader engages in this kind of question- ing, members experience themselves as objects; the leader re- lates to them as things to be manipulated, not as persons to be known.

It is probably more difficult for leaders to eliminate ques- tions from their own verbal behavior than it is to eliminate group members' questions. Leaders who give up questions may be giv- ing up their own method of control—their entire repertoire of group leadership techniques.

When Members Ask Questions of Each Other

To eliminate questions from members, the leader must insist that members rephrase questions into statements, making their position clear. The leader's responsibility is to intervene and insist that the member asking the question make a statement concerning his or her position, thought, or assumption behind the question. For example, a member asking another member, "Why didn't you ask the teacher for permission to leave the room?" might become, "I think you should have asked the teacher for permis- sion to leave the room." "Why" questions are accusatory and belong solely to the person making the statement. Refocusing the question opens the possibility for continued interaction be- tween the members.

Questioning is a common practice in social interaction, and group members see this as an acceptable form of behavior. Group members should be helped to "own" their questions, as ques- tions are always the agenda of the person doing the question- ing. The leader helps the questioner refocus on the self. It takes time for some members to refocus, but rarely is a member unable to respond and turn the question around so as to "own" the question. As a result, the tone of the group process changes, and members are more interactive. Here are two examples of how a group leader might refocus the discussion.

> *Sam:* Do you always get nervous when you have to speak before a group?
>
> *Leader:* I'm uncomfortable with you asking Paul a question. Instead, your question very likely has something to do with you. Can you speak for yourself?
>
> *Sam:* Yes, ah...when I have to talk before a group, I become so uptight I can't respond. I want to run away.

> *Peter:* Do you always feel like striking out when someone calls you a bad name?
>
> *Leader:* Peter, you have asked Kevin a direct question. It might be that your question has something to do with how you feel. Can you speak for yourself and respond to Kevin?
>
> *Peter:* Yes, ah...when I am called names, I want to just hit that person.

It is important for the leader to *always* refocus questions. In the examples above, the leader has helped the group members to "own" their feelings rather than working them out vicariously through someone else in the group.

When Questions Are Asked of the Leader

Sometimes benign questions are asked of group leaders—questions that have nothing to do with the process at hand. Examples might be "Are you married?" "How long have you been leading groups?" "Do you have children?" "Are you a doctor?" Some questions are so harmless that when answered by the leader they have no long-term effect on the group. Not all group members may want the information, but when the leader avoids responding because such information is irrelevant to the group process, some members may cease to self-disclose, resulting in an interruption of the group process. In his years of experience as a group leader, Friedman (1989) has found that answering without elaboration has never led to a disruption of the group process. However, responses to questions such as "What did you do last night?" "What are the names of your children?" are discouraged.

To eliminate questions from members, the leader must insist that members rephrase questions into statements, making clear their positions. The leader's responsibility is to intervene and insist that the member asking the question make a statement concerning his or her position, thought, or the assumption behind the question. For example, a member asking another member "Why didn't you ask the counselor for permission to leave the room?" might become, "I think you should have asked the counselor for permission to leave the room." "Why" questions are accusatory and belong solely to the person making the statement. By refocusing the question, the leader allows the possibility for continued interaction between members.

Warding off Gossip

Warding off "gossip" is far easier than deterring questions. To block questions, the leader must work against an ingrained speech pattern that involves a valued control of others. In situations involving gossip, members are talking *about* another member rather than directly *to* the member. For example, one member may refer to something that occurred, or a reaction, or a concern that involves another member, and addresses still another member, or the group as a whole. In such a situation, the leader should intervene and ask the member to speak directly to the other member concerned.

Leaders' interventions to block gossip are inherently inconsistent. When they direct one member to speak directly to another member, rather than speaking about him or her, leaders are themselves speaking *about* the other member. This problem seems imbedded in the English language and appears to be a necessary case of "Don't do as I do, but as I say" on the part of the intervening leader. One way to handle this inconsistency is to call the group's attention to the necessity for the leader's intervention being stated in the third person while asking members to communicate in the first person. Here are two examples of leader interventions to stop gossip.

> *Joe:* Pete, I am mad at you now for doing those silly things.
> *Bill:* Joe, I am mad at Pete too.
> *Leader:* Bill, you are talking *about* Pete. Please talk directly to him.
> *Bill:* Pete, I am mad at you, too, and would like you to quit doing the things that you later regret.

> *Mary:* John didn't really mean what he said, I'm sure.
> *Leader:* Mary, would you please speak directly to John.
> *Mary:* John, I don't think that you really meant that comment to be destructive.

Controlling Invasions of Privacy

One of the major functions of leaders is to protect the privacy of members. In addition to parrying questions, the leader also anticipates the climate and suppresses content that may invade privacy. In adult groups, members can safely volunteer materials from their own life-spaces and can exercise personal judgment concerning what to bring to the group and can determine for themselves what they wish to avoid.

When a group consists of minors drawn from a school setting, the protection of privacy becomes more complex. Students should have their family's privacy as well as their own protected, but young people frequently do not have the judgment to know whether content is appropriate to bring to a group. Leaders must be alert to any content that may damage group members or their families, particularly in the school setting. For example, if a student group member who is a minor brings up a concern regarding sexuality, the leader can prevent extensive elaboration of the content. The leader can focus on how the student feels about this particular issue, rather than going into details about particular events.

If a student group member describes a parental quarrel, the content should not be pursued; the privacy of the mother and father should be protected. Leaders should focus on the concern and feelings members are experiencing in the here-and-now. For example, when a group member became upset as she began to describe a bitter fight between her parents that she had witnessed before leaving for school, her voice faltered and she appeared to be suppressing tears. Instead of allowing the member to describe the intimate and awful details of her experience, the group leader redirected her awareness to what she was experiencing at the moment she was speaking.

> *Leader:* You must have some pretty bad feelings to have two people fighting who are very important in your life. Can you tell us what your feelings are right now?

The girl began to reveal her feelings of helplessness and despair. Others in the group described feelings they also experienced in situations that seemed similar to them; they need not have experienced strife in their own family in order to identify with feelings of helplessness and despair. Similar experiences are those that *produced* such feelings. Members connecting with each other in this way will enhance the group process, and the group will become more interactive as well as more cohesive.

Privacy is one of the major content differences in individual and group counseling. Areas dealing with family relationships, atypical sexuality, and discussion of people not present are *not appropriate* in an extensional group setting. They are appropriate for exploration in individual counseling. A general principle to follow is that exploration or discussion of any content that may later damage members or their families must not be encouraged in group. Here are two examples of a leader redirecting discussion away from inappropriate disclosures.

> *Sally:* My mother and father really got into it last night. He came home drunk as usual.
>
> *Leader:* I am reacting right now with some tension to your rapid speech and facial scowls, Sally.
>
> *Sally:* Yeah, I really feel uptight. I'm tense and would like to yell.

> *Jim:* I'm kind of mixed up. I had a dream last night that I was in a show and a gay person sat down next to me. I didn't know what to do.
>
> *Leader:* Dreams are sometimes confusing, Jim. Sometimes they seem very real. That dream was last night. How do you feel about it now?

Using Nonverbal Information

Nonverbal behavior is a particularly important source of information for group leaders. Alertness and sensitivity to nonverbal data can provide group leaders with a rich source of interactive material. The thumb tucked tightly inside a fist, a flexing jaw muscle, arms folded tightly across the chest, the drumming of an index finger, the selection of a floor cushion as a seat—these all represent important messages to group leaders. Although leaders may not always respond immediately to verbal or silent signals such as tight fists, drumming fingers, excessive yawns, inappropriate smiles, or a flushed neck, leaders observe and draw tentative meaning from them. When verbal and nonverbal cues seem incongruent, when the tone of voice insinuates one thing while the words say another, when lips are smiling but hands are clenched, the leader is watchful. The language of nonverbal communication in a group is rich with silent signals that can be received by a leader's sensitive antennae. The leader "hears" as many of these signals as possible, then responds selectively and in a responsible manner.

Group leaders also may note changes of posture, rates of speech, direction of gaze, length of messages and silences, and changes in facial expression. Group leaders need not be tentative about increasing their awareness of nonverbal group behavior. In most cases nonverbal clues are merely a source of information for the leader and are not a subject for discussion.

What can group leaders do once they have noted a specific nonverbal behavioral response in a group member? There are several alternatives. One is for leaders to offer their perceptions and feelings concerning the behavior in question. For example, if a member answers a question "yes" while at the same time shaking his or her head "no," the leader may feel confused by this contradictory set of responses and let the member know it. But remember that a perception of nonverbal behavior given by the leader or any group member is the personal feeling of the individual holding the view, and the person producing the behavior may choose to accept or reject this view.

Another alternative is the one leaders use most frequently. They simply note the behavior silently, storing it away as tentative information about the group member, using this added knowledge to make better judgments as they proceed with the group process.

Frequently group members are not aware of the nonverbal messages they are sending, and the question arises whether the leaders are indulging in psychological voyeurism when they observe and try to understand meanings behind their observations. When a leader first chooses to react verbally to a nonverbal cue, members may become self-conscious and uncomfortable, and these feelings should be discussed openly. Once members understand that nonverbal language is only an extension of verbal language, they can come to terms with the fact that they are transmitting messages constantly, consciously or unconsciously, and that these messages are being received constantly, consciously or unconsciously.

Nonverbal messages do not have universal meanings. Corey, Corey, and Callanan (1993) remind us that many cultural expressions are subject to misinterpretation. For instance the authors suggest that mainstream Americans may fill the air with words in their discomfort with silence, yet Japanese may place more value on indirectness and nonverbal communication, and Asians and Native Americans may view any direct contact as a lack of respect, including the typical direct eye contact mainstream Americans revere. Thus, we should become sensitive to cultural differences "to reduce the probability of missed communication, diagnosis, and misinterpretation of behavior" (Wolfgang, 1985, p. 100).

Although nonverbal behavior is an omnipresent factor of group counseling that everyone engages in all the time (Dyer & Vriend, 1980), the group leader must wait for the "propitious moment" to respond to nonverbal behavior. Here is one way a group leader might include nonverbal behavior in a group session.

> *Leader:* Joann, you seemed to react to Pete's pain as he was speaking, but you did not respond at the time. You had a pained look on your face, you pushed your chair back, and clenched your hands tightly as Pete talked. Perhaps the content of what he had to say was particularly troubling to you.

Here, the leader could ask either for feedback from Joann or from others in the group—asking them to explain what Joann's behavior meant to them. The main purpose of the leader's response is to help put Joann in touch with her nonverbal behavior and help her focus more intently on what it meant. The carefully worded response in this example would very likely have a positive effect on Joann.

Sometimes an ineffective leader will respond to nonverbal behavior in inappropriate ways. Here are two leader responses to avoid.

> *Leader:* I saw you smile when Gerald was denying those things about himself. Now tell him what was behind that funny grin.

> *Leader:* Mary, you are a bundle of nerves in this group. You shake when spoken to, you try to hide yourself by folding your arms in front of you, and you stutter when you speak. Now what's behind that nonverbal behavior? (Dyer & Vriend, 1980, p. 124)

Dyer and Vriend (1980) also provide an example of the leader misusing the data and attaching significance when there is no cause to do so.

> *Leader:* John, when Suzi mentioned her math teacher, you raised your finger, and then later when the same teacher was mentioned, your foot moved. This time when Mrs. Math Teacher was mentioned, you put your elbow in your ear. Now what's going on here, John? Your nonverbal behavior is giving you away. (p. 124)

It is important to remember that nonverbal messages cannot be read with certainty. To suggest that they can be is irresponsible, but to ignore them is equally irresponsible. However, Corey (1995) warns, "Group leaders would do well to avoid making bold interpretations—for example, that keeping one's arms crossed means that one is closed—and instead encourage members to merely pay attention to the nonverbal clues they emit" (p. 309).

While group leaders should observe as many nonverbal signals as possible, they need not respond to them verbally. Nonverbal information that has been "tucked away" may be useful later as the members' needs and characters unfold. Competent group leaders resist the folly of interpreting nonverbal data as if there were universal and permanent meaning for everyone. The measure of skill in this area is not how accurate leaders are with their perceptions and interpretation but how they use their observation in a tentative, caring, and inviting manner. Accuracy of interpreting nonverbal data is a distant second to the primacy of demonstrating interest and concern in the member.

Territoriality

Territoriality has more commonly been used to describe animal behavior, but it is also useful in understanding human behavior. Territoriality provides another nonverbal cue that can increase our understanding. People react to the physical proximity of others. They may not *always* move to or from something overtly to adapt to their attraction or discomfort, but a host of nonverbal cues emerge when personal space becomes an individual issue.

The amount of life-space group members unconsciously declare to be their territory may be observed by noting whether members move their chairs into the circle, shift closer to each other, or position themselves to allow maximum space between the chair or body and others in the group. In general, persons who maintain an unusually wide physical distance between their life-space and that of others are also likely to be more comfortable with the same psychological distance.

As leaders become sensitized to territoriality signals, they may note that a group member who chooses a corner is making a different statement from that made by one who chooses to sit on the floor at the foot of the leader. They might notice how subgroups arrange themselves. Do members group themselves in relation to various age groups? In relation to sexes? Who keeps the chair just outside of the group? Who wants more space between the chairs? All of these nonverbal choices carry meaning. Translating these verbal choices into meanings and the importance of these meanings are left to the sensitivity of leaders, who have to be aware of their own biases and limitations, which inevitably distort input.

Summary

Major leader interventions have been addressed in this chapter: deterring questions, warding off gossip, staying in the present tense, personalizing statements, avoiding super-mothering, forestalling mind-raping, and controlling invasions of privacy. Sometimes these interventions overlap and interweave, and sometimes they are discrete. The interventions described are observable to some degree in all interaction groups, even if the group leader's theoretical stance may be something other than extensional.

Issues related to nonverbal communication and ways leaders can use nonverbal information are also discussed. Observing the behavior and mentally recording the event may expand the leader's images of members. Nonverbal information that has been "tucked away" may be useful later as the member's needs and character unfold.

Competent group leaders must resist the folly of interpreting nonverbal data as if there were a universal and permanent meaning for everyone. The measure of skill in this area is not how accurate leaders are but how they use their perceptions and interpretations. Accuracy of interpreting nonverbal data is a distant second to the primacy of demonstrating interest and concern in the member.

6

Pathways to
Leadership

*At its core, therapy is a deeply human experience, and conse-
quently, there are an infinite number of pathways through the
therapeutic process.*

(Irvin D. Yalom)

Modeling

s modeling is a subtle, im-
perceptible, and elusive process, leaders of groups should be
aware that they model by their response mode, through their
attending behavior, through nonverbal cues, through quiet authority, and by exposing their compassionate spirit. Outside of
groups, individuals are greatly influenced by many others—sports
heroes, actors, musicians, teachers, professors. Models of various sorts influence the way we dress, assume our long-term goals,
and practice our profession. Within the group process, group
members are exposed to other group members as well as to the
leader. All are potential models. Thus, in an unstructured manner members set their sights on those whom they admire. "On
some level they imagine it possible that they, too, can assimi-
late those qualities they most admire" (Kottler, 1986, p. 16).

When a leader is performing the function of modeling, members may at times assume that the leader is being another member. When leaders transmit how it is with them, group members
are not always aware—and need not be aware—that the purpose is to provide a model of authentic interaction. It is not necessary for the members to differentiate between these roles, but

it is vital that leaders do so. That is, leaders must make it very clear by their behavior that they are not members of the group but that they do have feelings and reactions that when expressed to the group demonstrate their humanness and authenticity.

The modeling function involves a leader working in the framework of the extensional model, remaining in the here-and-now, avoiding use of questions, honoring and protecting the private life-spaces of members, emphasizing positive elements rather than negative elements, and being authentic and open. Leaders also model the verbal vehicles that make group processes unique—confrontation and feedback. They teach by example how to be a group member. Here are two examples of leaders performing modeling behaviors in group interactions.

> *Gerry:* I really react to you, Ann, when you smile. It makes me feel warm and accepted.
>
> *Leader:* Yes, I can relate to that Gerry. I respond the same way, Ann. When you smile at me, I feel recognized and legitimized.

> *Joe:* I like people very much, and I want to be liked. I find it hard to talk to people I don't know.
>
> *Mary:* I was wondering if you were ever going to talk, Joe.
>
> *Leader:* Joe, I feel good that you participated in the group tonight. I like hearing about your feelings.

Communication Patterns to Avoid

Certain speech behaviors are not helpful in communication in group. Questioning has already been discussed as being hostile and as a way of controlling others. Interpreting can be a form of mind-raping, which should be avoided in the extensional model. Calling attention to the group process is not helpful, because it tends to make an object out of the group and thus of group members. We suggest that leaders avoid talking about the process itself with the group except when training leaders. Summarizing is seldom helpful. This speech pattern "places a period on communication," which may inhibit growth. Instead of summarizing, group leaders might routinely "cap" at the end of each session (see Chapter 4). Speech patterns of "I hear you saying..." are irritating and often represent mind-raping. Sentences beginning with "You feel..." "You are feeling..." can be patronizing, and they also may represent mind-raping. Efforts to elicit a "because" answer or an answer to a "why" are not helpful.

"Should" and "should not," "don't worry," "I was there, too," "I understand how you feel because...," "I coped with it, so you can" are all speech patterns that must be avoided by group leaders. Members may exhibit these verbal behaviors, but leaders should not.

Straight comments, clear positions, risk of self, and I-to-Thou verbalizations are helpful. When leaders function as communication facilitators, they model these speech patterns.

Leader Transparency

Leader transparency (self-disclosure) is also a form of modeling. Being transparent requires an active response (when appropriate) to "at the moment" feelings the leader may experience during the group process. For instance, the leader might say one of the following, "I liked the way you said that," "I'm glad you could express how you felt," "Now I know more about you, and I like what I know," "I'm touched by your tears." A wise leader does not express negative feelings if they have no real purpose in assisting a group member. Here is an example of a leader intervention that is *not* to be encouraged. Avoid this kind of intervention in response to a group member having spoken in anger to another member.

> *Leader:* I am uncomfortable with the method by which you responded. It makes me want to be angry with you.

Instead, a skilled group leader might intervene in this way.

> *Leader:* I sensed your anger. Can you talk about what you were experiencing when you made that response?

When used improperly, transparency can become problematic for the leader if group members escalate their needs and cajole the leader into revealing more than is required. Also, despite group members asking for more leader self-revelations, group members are really not interested in information about the leader other than what pertains to the group. An unknown leader is a more powerful leader.

Evaluating the Message

Reflecting Content and Feelings

Much of the discussion that takes place in group interaction should have a focus if members are to become aware of meanings and implications. The leader can reflect content, rephrasing material in fresh, new words, capturing the essence of the statements so that members can hear more accurately their own words and the verbalizations of others. Here is one example of a leader reflecting content.

> *Avis:* You might not show it right out. You may think you despise your parents and might tell everybody you hate them, but deep down you actually know you really love your parents. Kids under 18 have to have someone over them, and they actually are afraid of losing that, but they don't really know it.
>
> *Leader:* ...afraid of losing the security of having someone responsible for you.
>
> *Avis:* Yes, all kids need someone to tell them what to do.
>
> *Leader:* It sounds like you're saying, Avis, that you appreciate having someone older help you make decisions at times.

Anyone trained in a nondirective stance is adept at reflecting feelings. The response, though difficult to learn, becomes almost automatic once it is learned. The danger of this verbal response pattern is that it can become trite and parrot-like. A group leader must be sensitive and verbalize feelings accurately and be careful not to mind-rape in the process. Here is how one leader chose to reflect feelings in a group interaction.

> *Greg:* I really don't want to lose Shirley, but I simply don't know what I can do to prevent it from happening.
> *Leader:* ...and that's a pretty helpless feeling.
> *Greg:* That's it—helpless. I'd be willing to do almost anything to keep her interested in a close relationship. But then, sometimes I get the feeling that it all has been pretty one-sided, with *me* making all the effort.
> *Leader:* It's like a double bind for you. You want Shirley badly but not at the price of losing your self-respect.

Speaking Congruently

One of the goals of a group leader is to help members reduce their possible inhibitions about self-disclosure. Telling another person exactly what is on your mind at all times is not what is being proposed here. Sometimes, cruelty has been passed off as "being honest" or "telling it like it is." An extensional group is an appropriate environment for self-disclosing and providing feedback to others in the form of congruent messages. In a congruent message the speaker expresses his or her internal feelings and perceptions as truly and as completely as possible while experiencing them. This is a message in which observable behavior and verbal reports match.

A common tendency is to suppress or conceal feelings, to make less than a complete report of what is happening within us. We tend to label other persons instead of expressing feelings and perceptions and assuming responsibility for them. When someone says, "You're neat!" it probably means, "I feel good when I'm with you." "You're evasive" (a label) could really mean, "I'm frustrated by my lack of success in making contact with you."

Congruent messages, then, are attempts to speak authentically in the here-and-now. Risks are involved. The person to whom you are attempting to be congruent may not accept what you are saying. To have our good intentions misinterpreted does not feel good. But withholding a congruent message to avoid risk does nothing to enhance meaningful communication and interaction. The group leader must model congruent speaking and be alert to recognize when it is happening with group members. The skill of congruent speaking is important to the group process, particularly when confrontation is involved.

Perception Checking

Perception checking is an attempt to see if another person's feelings are as you think they are. This is certainly important for group leaders in terms of confirming their intuition and in modeling appropriate group behavior for members. Perceptions are influenced by what is said and observed. Group members must have opportunities to express their perceptions so they may be confirmed, adjusted, or rejected. Misperceptions lead to prejudices and distortions. Here is an example of how two group members addressed this issue.

> *Jim:* Pete, you seem angry with me. You have been very quiet since I shared my feelings with you.
>
> *Pete:* No, I'm not upset. I have been thinking about what you said a few minutes ago. I need time to sort it out in my mind.

Had Jim not checked his perception with his fellow group member, the misperception may have remained as interference between them.

Leaders will also perception check what they have gleaned from a member. By doing so, the leader may interpret a feeling to a member who is not aware of what is being expressed. The leader's response is not definitive. Instead, it is a way to check what the member may or may not be experiencing. The leader's response most often moves the member to a higher level of personal insight.

> *Leader:* Susie, I believe you are experiencing a great deal right now. I sense a feeling of worthlessness on your part. Do I have that right?

In another example, as June revealed her feelings about a possible separation from her husband she began to cry. Pat, a fellow group member, also began to cry and with tears streaming down her cheeks, she grinned and said, "This is silly!" This started a dialogue about what Pat was feeling.

> *Ed:* I'm confused, Pat. What's silly? I can't tell if you're happy or upset.
> *Pat:* I'm upset! Any fool can see that.
> *Leader:* Pat, I'm having difficulty understanding also. Please, can you help us? You are obviously crying, but you looked as if you were laughing too.

In her response to the leader, Pat described how she identified closely with June as she relived the time when she divorced her first husband. Because she could not contain her tears in recalling an event that should have been long forgotten, Pat thought of herself as being foolish. "This is silly!"—"this" meaning her tears.

The leader's attempt to understand Pat's situation was an example of perception checking; that is, sharing an observation of what seemed to be Pat's feelings, and asking for clarification. Perception checking requires the courage to risk being misunderstood or misinterpreted. It is an invitation to share and confirm experiences. Although it is not limited to confrontation, perception checking is obviously a vital part of implementing confrontation as a strategy. And the value of checking positive perceptions should not be overlooked. They are as important to facilitating the group process as are negative perceptions.

Linking

The process of tying one member's comments to another member's comments may be helpful at times. The linking response may involve either ideas or feelings and may link verbal and nonverbal messages.

> *Jeanne:* The pressures of going to school, working and trying to live a healthy, balanced life are overwhelming me.
>
> *Leader:* That seems to have become a recurring theme in our group. Can you identify with anyone else in our group who might be experiencing your feelings?

What the Leader Sees

Observing nonverbal behavior provides valuable information for sharpening communication and group interaction. It has been said that we "tend to believe our eyes more than our ears"; that is, if we perceive incongruity in what we see and what we hear, we are likely to believe what we see. It is like the stage actor, bug-eyed and visibly shaking, he is asked, "Are you nervous?" In a quivering, squeaky voice, he quickly replies, "Nope!" as he continues to shake. The visible behavior seems more significant than his denial.

One caution is crucially important when using nonverbal cues in communication. This is rooted in the authors' existential philosophy that each person is ultimately responsible for themselves. One can speak only for oneself. This view conflicts with some of the popular literature on nonverbal communication (Fast, 1971; Knapp & Hall, 1992) that associates universal meanings with certain nonverbal behaviors. For example, locked thumbs in the belt directly above the pockets supposedly indicate male sexual availability; arms folded tightly across the chest are supposed to mean "closed to discussion." But it is possible that the man with thumbs in his belt does not know what to do with his hands and that the person with folded arms is cold. The advertising blurb for one popular book on nonverbal communication promises that you can "penetrate the personal secrets, both of intimates and total strangers" if you read the book (Fast, 1971). Even if it were possible to use nonverbal information to "penetrate" someone's inner life-space, such a practice would be unethical and would interfere with communication rather than enhance it.

A more practical application of nonverbal communication is to trust one's intuition as to what the cues are suggesting. The key is for observers to share what they are perceiving and to accept responsibility for having interpreted the cues as they have. Responsibility for the meaning of nonverbal cues remains with the observer, not the behaver. Risks are involved in offering a perception of another person's nonverbal behavior, just as they are in confrontation and perception checking. Recipients are free to do as they choose with the information. They can accept it, reject it, ignore it, qualify it, justify it, and so on. Recipients are responsible for determining what value perceivers' information is to them.

What the Leader Hears

The *eyes* of the leaders constantly monitor nonverbal communications within the group; the *ears* of the leaders constantly monitor verbal communications. This listening and hearing constitute the listening skills of leaders. They see, hear, feel, sort, discriminate, react, act. The ears of the leaders are antennae that pick up not only surface content but also meanings and implications that are not always apparent to the untrained listener.

The listening-responding feedback role of group leaders is based on a thorough working knowledge of personality theory. Background in the dynamics of human behavior must be part of the professional preparation leaders bring to groups. The following comments, it is hoped, will help identify possible areas of sensitive listening that might be processed by group leaders as they function as facilitators. We do not intend to provide a "listening cookbook" that can substitute for extensive background in psychological theory.

One major "listening post" for leaders who function in the extensional model is the explicit and implicit value hierarchies of each member. Participants can extend their life-spaces more effectively if they are aware of the value bases from which they operate. Leaders can use their listening skills to help members "hear" their value systems. As members interact, these systems are clearly disclosed and, when appropriate, leaders can provide feedback. Obviously, leaders avoid judgmental responses. The "goodness" or "badness" label attached to a value arises from a member. Leaders neither approve nor disapprove. Their task is to help members each "hear" their own values and become aware of their priorities. What members do with this knowledge outside the group is their own responsibility.

Adult participants, through their verbal and nonverbal expressions, indicate that they have internalized stances toward the traditional cultural values of work, achievement, "things," friends, cleanliness, honesty, learning, thrift, travel, and so forth, but they may be only dimly aware of how these stances have been translated into a unique lifestyle. Preadolescent and adolescent participants, through verbal and nonverbal expressions, may reveal their questioning of traditional cultural value systems. As they examine their own values, however, they may find that they are chiefly "reactive" rather than "proactive"—that is, *against* something rather than *for* something. The value of nonconformity, for example, requires a conformity against conforming, or a conformity of nonconforming. Group leaders use their listening skills to help participants identify their existent value systems and become aware of the accompanying implications for lifestyles.

Leaders listen, too, to life-space verbalizations about things members may wish to change. For instance, leaders may take particular note of expressions of inadequacy, incompetency, worthlessness, despair, expressions of "I'm not okay," and so on. These negative self-expressions probably represent elements participants would like to change in their personality functioning. Comments about feelings of rejection, whether it be of others or oneself, of wishes to "get even" or to be punished—in general, of deficiency needs—may point to areas members want to examine. Verbalizations of guilt feelings, feelings of loneliness, of isolation, or depression may indicate a "human nourishment" deficiency, and perhaps in group this deficiency could be relieved.

Again, leaders may or may not respond verbally to the content they "hear." They may only make mental notes of overt or covert expressions of a member's ambivalent, conflicted feelings about a significant other. A leader may only silently monitor expressions of members' neurotic needs to control and manipulate others. In the extensional model leaders are more likely to respond verbally to non-neurotic needs of creativity, self-expression, and enjoyment. In general, in this model leaders process both deficiency and growth needs, but they may respond verbally more frequently to the latter.

A thorough knowledge of defense mechanisms is essential for group leaders. Rationalizations, projections, intellectualizations, denials, and so forth may be data that a leader might process but not verbalize. The current developmental task that each member is addressing, however, probably will be identified to bring it into the member's awareness so that he or she can more actively cope with it.

The ears of the leader are acutely tuned to grammatical and speech-pattern cues to understanding a member's frame of reference. If a leader is to be of use to members in extending their functioning, the leader must understand that frame of reference. One way to do this is to pick up speech cues.

All statements beginning with "I" are important. "My," "mine," and "ours" should be distinguished if the speaker's frame of reference is one of undue possessiveness or of being self-responsible. "Shoulds" and "oughts" are significant other-directed speech patterns. Any statement qualified by "but," any statement seeking approval (such as "okay?" at the end of a statement), excessive verbiage, excessive questioning, sighs, excessive explaining, apologies, speech intonations and hesitancies, demanding, commanding, doubting, contradicting—all represent verbal cues that leaders process so that they can enter fully into the life-space of a member. The intent is not to violate life-space but to use professional skills to extend a member's life-space.

Summary

Numerous pathways to group leadership have been addressed in this chapter. These include modeling, leader transparency, reflecting content, reflecting feelings, speaking congruently, linking, and perception checking. These functions often overlap and interweave, and sometimes are discrete. Although the purposes and setting of groups vary, leader interventions are roughly the same in an extensional model. All group leaders perform some type of interventions; all group leaders model in some fashion; all group leaders facilitate communication in various ways. In this chapter we have suggested ways in which a leader can develop reasonable skill and self-assurance so as to expect a productive group outcome.

7

Co-Leadership
Issues

T he merits of co-leadership are constantly debated by practitioners, yet no hard research suggests that single leadership or co-leadership of groups is more productive. Benjamin (1978) suggests that co-leading is for experienced counselors; it is not for two neophytes who feel insecure in their roles and lack confidence in their interventions. The interpersonal dynamics between co-leaders are crucial to a successful group. The important issues to be considered in co-leadership are the theoretical orientation from which the leaders operate and the compatibility, mutual respect, and leadership styles of the personnel available. In this chapter we will discuss the merits of co-leadership as well as the disadvantages.

Advantages of Co-Leadership

Co-counselors who have had successful group leadership experiences find sharing leadership to be more satisfactory than single leadership. One satisfaction stems from the post-group critique; areas of concern, areas of success, and areas that need to be explored can be discussed by the co-counselors immediately after a session. Instant feedback can be given concerning the quality of the interventions of each leader.

Another satisfaction of co-leadership lies in the "anchor" one member of the team provides while the other member is engaged in intensive interaction with one or several members of the group. When one of the group leaders focuses very deeply

on the life-space of an individual member, the leader responding to a member may lose his or her monitoring of the group as
a whole. In the co-counselor model, the co-leader will monitor
the other group members.

A third advantage of sharing leadership is that it provides a
model of confrontation without risking a group member. Co-
leaders are expendable to each other, and they can use one another to model confrontation at a depth that might be unwise if
the interaction were taking place between the leader and an individual member.

A fourth asset of the co-counselor model is the constant
check each has for the other in respect to transference,
countertransferences, distortions stemming from biases, prejudices, weaknesses, and possible inaccuracies and shortcomings.
In the past, the psychoanalytical group spoke against co-leaders because of the belief that co-leaders severely inhibit the effects of the transference relationship, however Grotjahn, Kline,
and Friedmann (1983) are among those who rely heavily on the
transference process in groups today. The analytical group is
currently less united in their beliefs about the constraints of co-
leadership in respect to transference issues.

A fifth asset is that the productivity level of the group can
be maintained by the constant interaction of two leaders. Groups
with co-leaders tend to move rapidly and to sustain intense interaction throughout a session. Some leaders are more adept at
handling anger, depression, or resistance, while others may have
greater skill at being supportive. A major advantage of having
more than one group leader is the enhanced ability to penetrate
members' resistances and to quickly read significant affect-laden
material.

Finally, co-leaders reduce the strain on the attention span of
the leader. A single leader cannot pick up the innuendoes of all
individual group members at one time. Monitoring eight members, for instance, can cause a significant overload. Co-leaders
double the resources available to the group.

Kottler (1994) provides an example of the internal monitoring required of a typical leader.

> I've got to press Sandra harder. She's slipping away with her typical game-playing manners. Perhaps I could...Oops. Why is Rob squirming over in the corner? Did I hit one of his nerves? There go those giggling guys again. I better interrupt them before they begin their distracting jokes. Where was I? Oh, yeah. I was formulating a plan to motivate Sandra. But she keeps looking to Jody and Melanie for approval. I must break that destructive bond between them; they keep protecting one another. And there is Cary acting bored again, dying for attention. I've got to ignore him and get back to the problem at hand. But what is the problem at hand? (p. 190)

Disadvantages of Co-Leadership

No one would dispute the reality that counseling can be a lonely occupation. As in individual counseling, group leaders often feel isolated from others. Because of the demands of confidentiality and the safe haven that group work affords its members, the group leader cannot talk freely on the outside about group members. Even if the group counselor finds a colleague with whom to talk, finding someone whose clinical and theoretical underpinnings are compatible is difficult. In individual counseling, it is not hard to recognize a therapist from a particular theoretical system, such as cognitive behavioral, person-centered, rational/emotive, or the reality therapy point of view. Not so in group work. There are fewer "systems," and rarely can one find a "school" of individuals in a given geographical area with whom to consult. Therefore, finding a colleague with a similar theoretical frame of reference to share in the leadership is not too likely.

Despite the advantage of leading, and the stated support for co-leading (minus empirical data) by major authors and practitioners in group work, the emphasis in university training programs is still on the single leadership model. Why? First, counselors must initially learn to work alone. Second, training individuals in co-leadership is not cost-effective for most training institutions. Finally, learning to run groups takes time, and the university training program rarely has sufficient curriculum time to prepare co-leaders as intensively as individual leaders are trained.

Some counselors will agree with Shapiro (1978), who maintains: "It is my firm belief that every group can be conducted best by more than one therapist" (p. 157). Although this statement may have wide support, Carroll and Wiggins (1997) outline some of the common limitations of co-therapy:

- Competitiveness among co-leaders is common. Leaders may compete for member affection (like parents vying for the affection of a child). Or competition may develop when one leader, when challenged by the group, receives little or no support from the co-leader. Yalom (1995) cautioned apprentices to "avoid destructive competition as well as obsequious nonassertiveness" (p. 421).
- Most problems in groups run by co-leaders come as a result of unproductive relationships between the co-leaders. Each partner should supplement the other with a complementary style and technique. Co-leaders must be in synch with each other in respect to clinical interpretations, pacing, and response mode.
- Co-leaders may come to a point when they should cease to be together. Those who do not work well together should not continue to co-lead together.
- When a less experienced counselor joins a more experienced one as co-leader, the relationship is never equal.
- Co-leadership is not cost-effective. Can the institution, agency, school, or private practice afford to release two professionals to work with a small group? Finances can become a significant issue.

In sum, there is much to be found in the literature on co-therapy models, (Bowers & Gauron, 1981; Gans, 1962; McMahon

& Links, 1984; Russell & Russell, 1980), yet no one has provided any empirical evidence that co-therapy models are better. Hence, we cannot ignore Friedman (1989), who states, "In the absence of data, one may wonder why the co-therapy model persists and prevails" (p. 166).

Summary

The co-leader paradigm is still debated today. Reasons for the use of co-leaders are discussed in this chapter as well as the potential drawbacks of co-leadership.

Working with Difficult Group Members

Every collection of individuals, whether it be a meeting or a counseling group, will have at least one person whose behavior is disruptive or unproductive. Certain strategies can be employed, but before interventions are attempted, the leader must recognize the behavior, as well as its meaning. Because difficult group members can change the tempo of the group quickly, beginning group leaders may be caught unaware if they fail to notice the dynamics changing. Despite the need for an immediate response to the disruption, interventions must be attempted without assuming an authoritarian position that might chastise or demean the offending member. Trotzer (1989) and Shulman (1979) direct attention to coping with "problem" members in a firm but gentle manner.

Regardless of the setting, or the purpose of the group, most members of extensional groups participate voluntarily. The extensional group model can be used effectively in some nonvoluntary group situations, but for the moment we shall concentrate on voluntary groups. If the group's participants are present by choice, one would think that the leader's task would be relatively easy. Unfortunately, this is not always the case. Interpersonal needs are far too complex to permit a simple prediction of what to expect, even from a group of voluntary participants. Voluntary participation offers no guarantees for a smoothly running group.

Part of the leader's hard work is trying to assure that all group members are included as contributors to the group process. For the most part, members respond positively to the opportunity, but at times an individual member's resistive group behavior slows the process and inhibits others. The resistance does not have to be vocal or aggressive. Quiet withdrawal is also a form of resistance.

The member's resistance might be against the leader, against certain fellow group members, against the group as a collective body, or against taking responsibility for self. Resistance is manifest in many forms, and the motivation for resistance is complex. Moreover, detracting members may not even be aware of their resistance. Some members may have excessive needs for controlling others. They may fear losing self-control, fear the unknown, have a range of self-esteem varying from grandiosity to worthlessness, fear intimacy in any form, or may simply lack interpersonal skills.

For the most part, a leader should maintain objectivity when encountering resistance. Resistive detracting members probably are protecting themselves in some way, whatever form their behavior takes. If leaders are aggressive in their efforts to ameliorate the situation, this may legitimize the member's perception that he or she needs to protect the self.

The extensional group model assumes that individuals are responsible for themselves. Furthermore, it assumes that when individuals take responsibility for themselves, they maximize their potential for personal development. When group leaders confront detracting members, the leaders speak for themselves. The members can do what they wish with the information. Most important, leader confrontation is never done with the expectation that the person "shape up," as this goes against the principles of the extensional group. Finally, coping with a detracting member in a caring manner can be stimulating to the group process.

Difficulties in Expressing Feelings

A common challenge with group members is that some have difficulty expressing their feelings. How many times have we said "I feel" when what we have represented is not a feeling at all but, instead, a thought. For example, someone says, "I feel the Oakland A's are the best team in baseball." That is not a feeling statement. It is a thinking statement.

Feelings are intensely personal, often tentative, and once exposed, they can make us feel vulnerable. Group members may have difficulty expressing feelings either because they don't want to risk expressing them or because they are unaccustomed to expressing them. Difficulties with expressing feelings as they are occurring pose a specific problem in extensional group situations in which personal insights and growth depend on open communication of here-and-now feelings.

What often appears to be an unwillingness to communicate feelings may simply be an inability to identify feelings at a particular moment. And even if we recognize existing feelings, our vocabulary often limits our ability to communicate them. Expressing feeling as metaphors is sometimes helpful; for example, "I'm so confused I feel like I'm in a maze and can't find my way out." Another useful technique is to have members close their eyes and try to picture the feeling and then report the first impressions that come to mind.

Although the importance of expressing feelings is foremost in the group process, no one should be forced into expressing their feelings. If a leader can help a group member be open enough to say "I'm feeling pressured," that is a good beginning.

Specific Problems

Yalom (1995) declared: "I have yet to encounter the unproblematic patient, the patient whose course of therapy resembles a newly christened ship gliding smoothly down the slip into the water" (p. 369).

Some group members are suspected of having malevolent intentions. They may try the patience and compassion of the most skillful and dedicated group leader. The suggestions offered in the following pages as corrective or helping strategies have been most consistently effective for us. The reader is reminded that no group leader technique is guaranteed to be 100 percent effective. We admit that we have experienced failure at times, perhaps because we selected the wrong technique or strategy for the specific moment or the specific individual. More often, we have been able to explain our failures by recognizing that we were not aware of ourselves at that given moment.

The leader's self-awareness, sensitivity to others, and courage to act are far more critical in determining success than is the ability to accurately "categorize" individual group members and to employ the proper technique.

Members Who Cannot Talk in the Here-and-Now

The *here-and-now* simply means "the present moment." More often than not, leaders run groups dealing with issues, advice giving, and problem solving. In the attempt to take advantage of events, nuances, reactions, and unexpressed emotions within the group, an exclusive commitment to here-and-now emotions, feelings, and expressions is essential. A story of a past event, whether it be to seek advice or to discuss past experiences, is information central to the member describing the event. In the storytelling, however, fellow members are not participants and cannot identify with the particulars of what is being described. Therefore, the focus should be on the impact to the individual member of the event, the story, or a given dilemma.

In changing the focus, the leader may center on the affective elements and implement strategies for connections between members that bring the focus of the group to the present moment. The here-and-now approach, therefore, entails certain strategies and techniques that are easily described but difficult to carry out. The here-and-now has no beginning and no ending (Carroll & Wiggins, 1997).

The most effective mode for sustained, productive group interaction is that of helping group members talk in the here-and-now as much as possible. Although some members of groups are open and take pleasure in sharing personal anecdotes and tales in the group, this sharing of intimate information can lead to a common pitfall for beginning group leaders. In the desire to keep the group moving and get into meaningful interaction, the leader may be reinforcing nonproductive and potentially damaging behavior in the group. The problem with this kind of interaction is that some of the stories told include people not involved directly in the group. This does little to help group members interact with each other at the present moment. Even if the stories being related are about the person telling the story, they usually are founded in the past and thus acquire the nature of a third-person narrative.

If personal growth is to take place, the leader must help members focus on their feelings in the present. The leader can help accomplish this by listening to the story and reacting to the feelings, not to the specifics of the incident.

Imagine a high school student saying, "I hate Mr. Johnson. He's the worst biology teacher at this school. Do you know what he did? He refused to accept my paper because it was three days late, and that's going to be a major part of my grade. He really likes to flunk kids. He's unfair!" At this point, the leader has the option of focusing on Mr. Johnson, "Oh, you think he's really a hard-line teacher" or on the student's feelings, "You're not accustomed to being treated that way by a teacher, and it makes you feel angry and helpless."

Using the technique of focusing on here-and-now feelings, the leader has determined the direction of the group. The group either will be telling stories and airing grievances about unpopular teachers or it will be dealing with feelings of failure and frustration members might be experiencing.

Members Who Wait for Others to Speak First

Groups commonly have members who wait for others to speak or participate first, particularly in the early stages of group development. The behavior pattern of reluctant members usually falls into one of at least two types.

The first encompasses reluctant members who, through silence, exhibit what we have interpreted to be fear or anxiety about participating in the group. They feel that if they wait to be the last to speak, the group may overlook them, or perhaps time will run out, and thus they can avoid having the focus directed toward them. Individuals of this type are not necessarily opposed to being in the group. They probably enjoy the sense of belonging to and sharing in the experience. Consequently, they want to be a part of it, but they have an understandable anxiety about how to begin.

The leader can give these people a great deal of support. By respecting their silence, the leader allows them time to observe and become acquainted with the group process. The leader allows them to assess their own readiness to participate. Silence often stems from fear of being attacked, ignored, or rejected. Possibly silence is a means of avoiding the risk of feeling foolish or appearing dumb. The leader must be certain that a quiet member is not compromised in the group. If another member questions the member's silence, and in the leader's opinion the latter is visibly disturbed, the leader can direct the interaction to the group in general, asking something like, "Has anyone else found it difficult to get started?" or "Does participating in the group cause anxiety in anyone else?"

Many individuals who wait for others to go first have another common pattern of behavior. They simply rephrase what someone else has said already. Tom, a member, repeated what another member had said previously. Then Melinda retorted, "Tom, you always say what everyone else says. Don't you have a mind of your own?" Tom, obviously stunned and feeling attacked, replied, "Maybe someone else did say it, but it *was* my feeling."

This kind of exchange can go on indefinitely if the leader or another member does not intervene. Three intervening strategies are possible. In one, the leader can give support to Tom by affirming his participation. The leader could say something like, "Tom, I had the same feeling about John. I'm glad you saw it, too. Is there anything you can say to him that is different from what has been said already? What do you see in John that others might not see?" In this situation the leader has reinforced Tom's participation and also has allowed for his continued and more personal involvement in the group.

The second strategy is to intervene and direct the attention away from Tom and toward Melinda. Questioning is an indirect and unfair method of having another person share his or her feelings without risking one's own. By having Melinda restate her concern for Tom's participation, the leader can direct the group to the here-and-now and also have Melinda "own" her feelings rather than having Tom deal with an assertion of not having a mind of his own. The leader can intervene and say, "You seem upset by Tom's reaction. I would like for you to put your concerns into a statement rather than a question."

Another technique that has helped quiet members gain confidence is to use reaction papers, written after each group session. College-age groups in particular respond to this method successfully. Reaction papers summarize impressions and thoughts about the group experience. Quite often, reluctant members are willing to write the things they may feel inhibited about saying in the group. This gives the leader a form of self-disclosure, which usually strengthens the bond between member and leader. It also provides a low-threat means of expression. Too, reluctant members often say later in the group what they had written earlier in the reaction paper. The paper allows them an opportunity to formulate and "rehearse" their thoughts before expressing them verbally.

Silent Members

Carroll and Wiggins (1997) suggest that silent members appear in many forms. One is the person who rarely responds, and when he or she does, the response is so brief that it offers little to which anyone can react. Another is the person who is observing and taking it in. Still others may use silence as a form of manipulation. Some people are naturally shy, inhibited, embarrassed, fearful, or hesitant, and thus they appear resistant. The communication of silent members is often behavioral rather than verbal; they cannot put words to subjective experiences. A group member who is silent, for whatever reason, may block out all present experience, remain devoid of affect, and stare blankly throughout group interactions.

There is no best approach to provoking a response from a group member who persistently remains silent. When asked for a response, the response likely will be in the there-and-then, with nowhere to go once the statement has been made. For example, "I remember the last group I was in" is a there-and-then response, one that is "safe," as no one in the group can confirm the experience, or even desires to hear about it. Another dead-end response is, "I'm just listening to each person."

When leaders prod for a response to statements such as the ones above, the group dynamics change, and the member may gain control of the process. On the other hand, the member may be so conflicted by the probing that a response is unattainable.

A good rule of thumb is to refrain from initiating a direct response to the silent member. Rather, the leader observes the group response and uses strategies that require group members to respond to the individual member rather than the leader. Dealing with silent group members has no easy solutions.

Compulsive Talkers (Monopolists)

Many group leaders have suffered anguish when a member's endless chatter, interruptions, irrelevant stories, interrogations, filibustering, or identification with every group member's problems begins to control the group. The monopolizing compulsive talker often is among the first to speak in the initial group session. Although compulsive talkers appear to be the opposite of reluctant group members, in many instances their motivations are identical. Reluctant talkers and compulsive talkers both may be motivated by fear about participating in group activities.

To equate quantity of dialogue with authenticity of feelings would be erroneous. Dominating talkers often use excessive verbiage as a smokescreen to obscure their inability or unwillingness to really interact at a feeling level. It is as if they have said to themselves, "Well, they can't get me for not participating. If it's talking they want, I'll give them plenty." These are the most likely candidates to break silences or to fill in lulls in the interaction. Compulsive talkers frequently are storytellers, incident relaters, or gossipers. They probably will reply in an incredulous manner if someone observes, "You really haven't shared much of yourself."

The effect of the monopolist on the group is usually detrimental, as group members may react by making hostile remarks such as "shut up," "we've heard enough from you," and the like. If so, the leader must intervene immediately. The intervention should not be in the form of an attack, even though the monopolizer may perceive any response from the leader as a criticism. Ordinarily, groups can handle their own problems, but in the case of the monopolist, that person has gained control and the group has let it happen. As a result, the group is unable to handle the monopolist except by confrontation (Carroll & Wiggins, 1997).

Monopolists need to get feedback about their behavior. In most instances this helps them perceive themselves more realistically. Most important, "good timing is necessary; there is no point in attempting to do this work...in the midst of a fire storm. Repeated, gentle, properly timed interventions are required" (Yalom, 1995, p. 375).

Dependent Members

Leaders can make some fairly accurate judgments about a member's dependency needs if they observe revealing clues. Dependent members make frequent eye contact with the leader.

They actually may be talking with someone else in the group while looking actively for acknowledgment from the leader. A common indication of dependency on the leader is the member who talks to another member through the leader.

For instance, in talking about her boyfriend with whom she recently broke up, Maria says, "I could get him back any time I want." Linda, talking about Maria while looking at the leader says, "She's so arrogant about the fact that she can snap her fingers and boys will come running."

Assisting group members to speak directly to someone in the group requires members to send direct messages. It does not allow them to use the leader as a buffer or filter for statements they may fear risking.

Another characteristic of dependency is to restate or mimic the leader's own behavior. This is sort of a "me too" behavior. The leader says, "Don, I'm really pleased about the way you have shared yourself with us today." The dependent member comes right back with, "Yeah, Don, that's really neat," and then looks to the leader.

Although the leader may be the primary focus of a member's dependency, on occasion dependency may develop with other members. This behavior is similar to that of members who wait for someone else to speak first.

Some suggestions for dealing with dependent members are

- Be aware of dependency as it is developing. Do not reinforce it by allowing the dependent member to feed off the leader's approval. Try not to engage dependent members in eye contact when you suspect they are looking for affirmation. Be aware of subtle nods in the direction of these members that may be conveying approval.
- Share your observations and feelings about what is going on. Leaders not only should disclose their observations but also should check with others to see if their perceptions are comparable. If they are not, dependency could be an erroneous perception by the leader.

■ Attend to dependent members selectively, as the leader's attention seems to be reinforcing to them. Consciously look for ways to affirm indications of independent behavior, because that is a goal of growth and greater self-awareness.

Members Who Are Scapegoated

Scapegoating is one of the most common and frustrating problems for the group leader. Most often the person scapegoated is the object of displaced aggression. The initial task for the leader is to recognize scapegoating in the first place, then to act on it quickly, attempting to find the source of the aggression. Scapegoats have their own unique style. They may sermonize, be contentious, act dumb (not "getting" what everyone else understands), patter endlessly, ruminate about past events, or remain untouched by any appearance of intimacy.

Regardless of their unique style, scapegoats invariably become the focal point of negative feelings from group members. The negative feelings are generated by obvious inconsistencies between what the scapegoat says and what seems to be honest to the group.

Some leaders attempt to encourage group members to give feedback to the scapegoat, however Carroll and Wiggins (1997) feel that when sharing perceptions of the scapegoats' behavior, members may unload their aggression and vent their negative feelings on the scapegoat. When this occurs, group cohesiveness may shift to group hostility, taking various and subtle forms. (Hostility is more evident in adult groups than in groups with young children and adolescents.) Therefore, the leader's strategy of inviting perceptions and feedback about dishonest talkers should be employed cautiously. Although most group members unload on the scapegoat to vent their negative feelings, some members attack to prevent themselves from becoming the focus of the group.

Inexperienced group leaders often allow the focus to remain on the scapegoat because it assures interaction. Concentrating on the scapegoat for a long time is unproductive and actually could be harmful to the scapegoated member. Consequently, as negative as the reactions may be toward the scapegoat, the leader is responsible for seeing that the scapegoat's rights as a group member are not violated. Reminding members to use congruent messages should keep the group at a reasonable level of integrity.

Quite often the silent members are inclined to sympathize with or support the scapegoat. At least they may be thinking something that is nonattacking but are reluctant to become a vocal minority. They may need the leader's encouragement to express their thoughts to the scapegoat.

By observing nonverbal indications of concern, such as shifting positions, tense posture, and frowns, the leader can become sensitive to members who are withholding their feelings and thoughts. The leader might ask group members to focus on how they would feel if they were in the scapegoat's place.

Leaders also should recognize the difference between members' coming to the aid of the scapegoat because he or she actually has been wronged versus behavior that is more akin to super-mothering or "first aid." In the first-aid situation a member constantly runs to someone's (anyone's) defense to distribute "Band-Aids." By protecting the aggrieved person, first-aiders feel they also are protecting themselves from attack sometime in the future.

When analyzing the problem before them, leaders should look at their own feelings. If they have an urge to protect the scapegoat, what began as a problem between the group and the scapegoat may become a problem of the leader, the scapegoat, and the group. In these cases the group no longer has a leader. On the other hand, if the scapegoat is irritating not only to the group but also to the leader, the conflict becomes one of leader and group versus the scapegoat.

Sometimes group members attack a scapegoat because that person reminds the attacking members of things they do not like in themselves. Shulman (1979) provided the example of youngsters who are having trouble in school and described how peers pounce on every defect they can find in a group member who is experiencing the same problems—perhaps more severely, yet the same. The leader should avoid siding with either the scapegoat or the group, while each member must be helped to recognize the meaning of his or her behavior. Cohesive groups are able to freely express negative feelings toward themselves and the leader. When scapegoating occurs, group cohesiveness is endangered or possibly destroyed. Scapegoating, therefore, can be hazardous when unchallenged.

Challenging the Leader's Authority

Group behavior of hostile group members is extremely varied and complex. Group members who challenge the leader sometimes are subtle, such as "suggesting" how the leader could be more effective. At the other extreme is the overly belligerent, hostile member who directly attacks the leader's responsibilities and capabilities.

Challenges often come around the third or fourth session. In early sessions of the group, members view the leader as a source of expectation, authority, and gratification. Respect for and dependence upon authority is the societal norm. Most people view leaders, superiors, bosses, members of the clergy, police, government, and parents as authority sources. In transferring this norm to the group process, group members usually expect the leader to start each session and to present topics for discussion. As the group process moves on, however, members will begin to challenge the leader by making statements such as: "I didn't like the way you pressured Jane," "I don't like what you said," "I don't like the way you did that."

The basic message for leaders coping with a challenger is to "stay cool." Leaders should model self-disclosure for the group, expressing here-and-now thoughts and feelings authentically. They should resist the urge to put down the challenger. Leaders should remain objective, with the assumption that the challenger is seeking to protect himself or herself for some reason.

Keeping "cool" in the face of a member's challenge—whether subtle or direct—is easy to write about, but when the challenge actually arises, the leader's heart may beat faster and the muscles may tighten. The leader understandably might become absorbed with coping rather than leading. Rather than pretend that nothing has happened or to try to suppress the challenger and force compliance, a supportive response informs the member that the leader has made no conscious attempt to be hostile or controlling. A response might be, for example, "I'm glad you can tell me that." This in no way implies that the leader is going to discontinue his or her facilitating techniques as a leader. The leader really is communicating in a subtle manner, "It's okay. I still care about you. I can handle your hostile remarks."

The leader never should let a personal confrontation or challenge to authority go by. Because not all group members respond to authority in the same form, the leader should be looking for whatever form it takes. Response to authority occurs in all groups. Challenges to the leader must not become a hidden dimension of which the leader is ignorant.

Absentee Members and Latecomers

A member who is frequently absent is sending a strong message that some form of resistance is taking place. Trotzer (1989) observed that one good way of avoiding the therapeutic impact of a group is simply not to show up. Although they may be physically absent from the group, absent members are not forgotten. For the group members present, there is no such thing as "out of sight out of mind" (Trotzer, 1989).

Some members should just not be in the group. Because the leader's first priority is to maintain group integrity, the leader may have to remove the chronic absentee from the group. When this happens, group members may become defensive as they see the possibility of the same thing happening to them (whether they are or are not chronic absentees). The leader must remain firm in the decision to remove a group member. When opinions differ, group members will have an opportunity for a productive here-and-now dialogue.

When a group member is removed, that person should be given an alternative way to seek help, usually in the form of individual counseling. The group member should not see this recommendation in a pejorative sense but, rather, as an intent to still help the client, on a one-to-one basis with the leader or with someone to whom the person has been referred.

Lateness, like absenteeism, is disruptive. How many times have we heard, "My car wouldn't start" or "I had to go to the dentist" or "The baby sitter didn't come on time." How does the leader handle this? Should he or she ignore the latecomer, start on time, and risk losing the member by holding the line? The best way to curb lateness is to start! After the latecomer arrives, the leader should not recap the content of the session or respond to the latecomer's reason for being late. The group has begun already. Because the cause of lateness may have something to do with the group itself, the leader should attempt to find out the reason for the member's behavior.

Like the absentee, if lateness is chronic, dropping the member from the group may be necessary. Different from the chronic absentee, however, the leader may want the group to discuss the matter before a final decision is made.

Summary

Difficult members need not be conscious or deliberate in their actions. Their behavior can detract from the group's effectiveness quite innocently. Nevertheless, if their behavior is not addressed, the group experience can be diminished for everyone. In the extensional model, difficult behavior is viewed generally as a defense mechanism. Detracting members are attempting to protect themselves in some way.

The leader's task is to channel the occasion to benefit the detracting member as well as the group if possible. The leader's reaction to the detracting member is likely to be shared by others in the group, and the leader should encourage their expression. The leader's responsibility is to be honest with his or her own reactions, help others express their feelings and reactions, and be considerate of the detracting member so everyone in the group has an opportunity to learn from the experience.

9

Verbal and
Nonverbal
Activities to
Promote
Interaction

Introduction to Structured Activities

Group leaders should not expect group members to know group process skills or to have a natural sense of what to expect. Few experiences in our lives even begin to approach the group experience. The skills required to interact quickly and productively in the unique situation that is group are quite different from those that keep social interactions comfortable. In everyday social intercourse, polite consideration for another's feelings is essential. Censoring feelings and reactions is necessary in most employment situations. Without basic good manners we could not live and work together in harmony. Of course, it is also naive to think that authenticity in group implies blurting out *every* "gut level" response the moment it comes to mind.

In ordinary interactions we present only a portion of our multilevel selves, or only a portion of our many roles as worker, parent, offspring, companion, lover, and friend. We all must censor some of our reactions and interactions if we are to remain functional.

Group is something else. Here, as leaders, we ask participants to forgo the normal social habits that are essential outside the group. We ask members to temporarily give up customary politeness, refrain from censoring, and respond to other group members with spontaneity. We ask members to report their feelings, thoughts, and spontaneous reactions to each other freely and fully without being concerned about the usual social rituals. We ask members to interact with each other at a level that would be awkward if maintained consistently in the world outside the group. With even the most trusting group member, these can be difficult requests. For members who are less trusting, more inhibited, or resistive, these requests can be formidable.

A Cautionary Note

The fundamental question is, how do we encourage group interaction? The conventional response has been through the various forms of intervention techniques discussed earlier in this book. What follows may seem in direct contradiction to the earlier discussions in this book. That is, we shall present a series of catalysts (exercises) that leaders may use to encourage group activity. These exercises are under the direct control of the leader and must be used skillfully and discriminately. Thus, before we describe the various structured exercises, we feel it is imperative to state at length why structured exercises can be the *least* desirable form of "forced" interaction; they are to be used sparingly and with wisdom. Although we suggest caution, it is not uncommon for group leaders to use these exercises one time or another in group situations that are less dynamic, such as small group instruction, task groups, or guidance groups. In such cases, group activities may be among the necessary armamentarium of the group leader.

Opening every session with a structured exercise or indiscriminately including an exercise during each session is questionable. Leaders who rely primarily on activities to maintain (rather than stimulate) interaction are certainly not skilled. The value and purpose of some exercises may be misinterpreted because they are light, active, fun, and sometimes mistaken for "parlor games." The leader is responsible for determining the group's level of emotional intensity. Skilled applications always require the leader to have a clear purpose in mind, an abiding respect for the members' rights to refuse to participate, and a sense of timing to determine when the structured activity should yield to natural interpersonal contact.

Thus, a leader's insistence on using or completing an exercise may actually detract from spontaneous interaction. The exercise is always secondary to the interaction it stimulates. Furthermore, activities are not inherently valuable in themselves; they do not assure meaningful interaction. A skillful leader is required to accomplish that. Carroll and Wiggins (1997) advise that a leader can misuse structured exercises in an attempt to draw group members into a dynamic interaction. Instead of doing the hard mind work of conceptualizing the here-and-now aspects of the group, the inexperienced leader may grasp for a technique without focusing on the process.

Another pitfall is that leaders commonly use structured exercises in the early stages of the group in an attempt to bypass the frustration of getting started. In later stages of the group, a leader may use exercises to accelerate the pace of the group. More often than not, whether used early or later in the group, the pace *is* accelerated, but in doing so, the leader gambles. Yalom (1995) described the consequences of hastening the process: "The exercises appear to plunge the members quickly into a great degree of expressivity, but the group pays a price for its speed; it circumvents many group developmental tasks and does not develop a sense of autonomy and potency" (p. 445). The group loses its sense of autonomy because the exercise becomes the focus of the group. In addition, a new process norm is introduced, prescribing that the leader will do the work of the group when the process bogs down.

Further, structured exercises reinforce dependency, placing the focus on the leader as well as putting the leader in the position of becoming the prime helper. As a result, group members become less inclined to help each other. Yalom (1995) stated that dependency upon structured exercises may cause group members to "deskill themselves and divest themselves of responsibility" (p. 447).

Sometimes, rather than accelerating the pace, the affective

elements of the group slip by and the group reaches a dead end. When a dead end is the result of a condition the leader created (the exercise), the leader is forced to assume responsibility for the group and deal with the consequences of the exercise.

Finally, members may be pressured or even feel coerced to respond to an activity. Shapiro (1978) strongly advocated timeliness, appropriateness, and member consent as basic conditions when using structured techniques. Carroll and Wiggins (1997) believe that in the long run the group process without structured exercises provides a learning climate that is more productive because members are more able to assume their own agendas than when the leader controls the process.

Although extensional groups are concerned primarily with interactive components, if the group engages in nonverbal exercises, the very nature of group work implies sharing and offering each other feedback during and after an activity. Spontaneous use of interactive activities is preferred over preplanned, highly structured exercises. Therefore, the activities in the following pages intentionally exclude those that require equipment (e.g., masks, slides, paints, videotape, and so forth). Paper, pencils, and pieces of construction paper are the only exceptions.

These activities vary in their potential for stimulating interaction. Some are patently low-keyed; others are designed to evoke interaction of great intensity. Although quantifying an activity's potential is difficult, an attempt has been made to estimate each activity's potential in terms of low, medium, or high intensity. A simple exercise may, for some reason, become surprisingly powerful in generating feelings within a person or within the group. In contrast, "heavy" activities may help some members go very deep while other members may feel little or nothing. The lesson is that structured activities are not always dependable.

Using high intensity exercises early in the group is discouraged. A reasonable amount of interaction is required before the bonds of trust begin to develop among members. The leader's skill, sensitivity, and courage are the major influences in determining success when using exercises. The reader can appreciate the possibility of accurately predicting on an a priori basis how effective an activity will be. The site, group purpose, and relative maturity of the group's participants are crucial considerations for determining the "right" exercise for the "right" moment.

Categorizing Structured Activities

The literature on counseling, human relations training, interpersonal communications skills, encounter groups, and the like offers a cornucopia of techniques and procedures that can be adapted as catalysts for an extensional group. We do not pretend to begin to cover the vast resources available to the reader. However, we will provide a framework in which to organize activities. To approach the use of activities intelligently so that objectives for using them make sense, it is necessary to have some means of organizing the flood of possibilities available.

In addition to the framework, a sampling of activities is presented. We do not offer them because they are the "best." In fact, we are convinced that leaders who look for techniques and procedures to assure interactive success in group are approaching their work naively. Techniques and exercises are only as good as the leader applying them. The leader's skill lies in the ability to adapt and adjust according to the demands of the moment.

A model for categorizing communication exercises is presented in Figure 9.1. Verbal and nonverbal distinctions are aligned in relation to *inter*personal and *intra*personal focus and amount of leader control. Table 9.1 presents information on the intensity to be expected with various exercises. The activities described in this chapter are organized into two major categories: *inter*personal verbal and nonverbal activities and *intra*personal verbal and nonverbal activities. Interpersonal activities involve interacting with other group members in dialogue—for example, introducing oneself to the group and answering questions. If the activity is nonverbal, words are not used, such as in the exer-

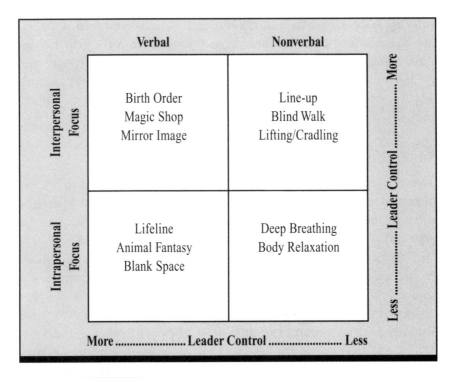

FIGURE 9.1

Categorizing Activities for Extensional Groups

Source: Adapted from Trotzer (1989), *The Counselor and the Group: Integrating Theory, Training and Practice* (2nd ed.). Muncie: Accelerated Development, p. 420.

cise "changing seats." Intrapersonal activities are those in which an exercise is done alone at first and then shared and explored with others at a later time, such as drawing a "lifeline" to be shared. The drawing is completed alone; the explanation of it is verbal. Nonverbal activities include private, personal experiences such as body relaxation.

Leader Control

A brief explanation about leader control is in order before proceeding to an examination of structured activities. In the extensional model the leader is *always in control* of the group pro-

TABLE 9.1

Level of Intensity of Selected Communication Exercises

Interpersonal Verbal Activities

low intensity	*medium intensity*	*high intensity*
birth order	strength bombardment	farewell
territoriality	self-report	mirror image
first memories	metaphors	legitimizing
free association	significant moment	
druthers	as a group member	
symbolic substitution	freezing	
new names	magic shop	
best possible way of life	role playing	
pair and share		
labeling		
three adjectives		
appreciate-regret		
true-false		
color cards		

Interpersonal Nonverbal Activities

low intensity	*medium intensity*	*high intensity*
line up	mill-in	lifting
hand mirroring	two-foot square	cradling and rocking
changing seats	blind walk	territoriality
	trust	nonverbal go-around
	break-in	feeling space

Intrapersonal Verbal Activities

low intensity	*medium intensity*	*high intensity*
lifeline	childhood	gestalt chairs
perfect day	rediscovery fantasy	twenty-four hours to live
	animal fantasy	new ways of behaving
	autobiographies	five roles
	symbolic objects	
	what would you like to be remembered for?	

Intrapersonal Nonverbal Activities

low intensity
deep breathing
body relaxation

cess. By "leader control" we are referring to the degree of overt action to be observed. The more-to-less continua in Figure 9.1 represents the relative amounts of intervention and facilitation in which the leader engages. The more *intra*personal and non-verbal the activity effects are, the less "material" there is for a leader to work with (control). The leader's influence is most visible when there is *inter*personal dialogue. In this model, leader control is a function of having something to control rather than meeting responsibilities for control. However, the "more" does not mean a leader should consciously exert increased control just because the model is dictating "more."

The extensional model creates an almost paradoxical leadership condition. The existential philosophy from which the extensional model was derived insists that each of us is ultimately responsible for ourself; yet we have emphasized repeatedly that the leader must never relinquish responsibility for controlling the group process. *How* leaders exercise control is the issue, not whether or not they should control. For example, leaders trying to create an encouraging environment for member self-responsibility may intentionally become less visible. It may appear, in fact, that the leader is doing nothing and allowing the members to direct events. Leaders who have created such an environment in the group are still in control. When introducing an exercise, competent leaders are clear in their intention to gradually withdraw and let members assume responsibility. Although such action may resemble abdication, it is definitely not relinquishing control.

Interpersonal Verbal Activities

Low Intensity

Birth Order. A simple but usually productive device to encourage group members to look at themselves is to ask the group to subdivide into small groups according to whether the member was first born, last born, or middle born. Members of each group discuss problems that occurred in their lives as a result of their sibling position. Then the entire group reassembles to share points of view. This technique focuses attention on present perceptions of group members as they talk about a productive topic of group content—individual members.

Territoriality. Asking a group that has been in session at least twice to change seats after the group has started will bring up the import of territoriality. Did group members tend to arrange themselves in the same seating order each time? How did they feel when they saw someone else sitting in their "territory?" Who sat next to whom after the rearrangement? What is each member's psychological territory? Acceptable social distances might be discussed before focusing on how close to some group members other specific group members can sit without becoming uncomfortable.

First Memories. Members share with the group their first memories of conflict. What was significant about those memories? Do group members perceive similarities in current behavior patterns that might create conflict?

Free Association. Free association can stimulate confrontation. The usual procedure is for the group leader to present a stimulus word that may or may not be "loaded" and ask group members to respond quickly around the circle. (The leader should note split-second censoring and perhaps call it to the group's attention.) This technique tends to bring out affective content and is useful as a warmup process. "Going-around" is seldom completed more than a time or two before the group is dealing with significant materials.

Druthers. The go-around begins with the sentence stem: "If I had my druthers, right now I would be..." This fantasy may help members explore their value systems, action choices, and self-acceptance.

Symbolic Substitution. Asking each member to fantasize what animal or bird or building or geometric figure or plant or color he or she would like to be is often productive as members crystallize their perceptions of who they are. In using this exercise, each member must direct the symbolic substitution to self; members should not be permitted to label other members as an animal, or whatever.

New Names. Another helpful way of exploring the sense of self is to have members each select a new name for themselves to be used in that group session. The group is asked to react to those names. Again, members should select their own names; others should not choose for them.

Best Possible Way of Life. Asking members to describe their best possible way of life and then, perhaps, their worst possible way of life, may help them identify where they are now on this continuum.

Pair and Share. In an excellent get-acquainted activity if participants in first sessions are strangers, the leader instructs members to each find one other person they would like to get to know. The pairs have approximately ten minutes in which to get acquainted. They are then instructed to find another pair they think might be interesting. The leader should allow sufficient time for members to introduce their partners to the other pairs.

Labeling. An enjoyable way for group members to learn each other's names in an opening group session is to have them select an adjective or descriptive label that precedes their name—for example, "I'm Studious Stan," "I'm Beer-Drinking Phil," "I'm Nervous Betty." A variation of this exercise is to go-around the group, with members stating as many previously offered labels and names as they can before revealing their own.

Three Adjectives. In a go-around procedure, each member is asked to describe himself or herself using three adjectives. The group interacts as each member offers these descriptive adjectives.

Appreciate-Regret. This exercise can be used constructively at various stages of the group's development, from beginning to closing. It is a semistructured activity that gives members permission to express themselves in the here-and-now. When a session has been centered for a long time on one individual, or the group has dwelt a long time on one theme or topic, the "appreciate-regret" activity allows all members to contribute something, however brief. The task is simple. Members are free to make as many statements as they wish that begin with, "I appreciate..." or "I regret..." This may be confused with *capping* (see Chapter 4). The difference lies in the activity's time perspective. Capping is designed to bring members' focus away from the here-and-now by reviewing thoughts and impressions that have taken place in the group in preparation for closing. In contrast, this activity focuses on *present* thoughts and feelings as they occur.

True-False. This go-around activity permits self-disclosure and feedback in an indirect way. Someone (usually the leader) starts by describing something about himself or herself that may be either true or fabricated—for example, "I have appeared in movies" (followed with details). When finished, other group members react with their judgments as to whether the person has told the truth or not. The important part of this exercise is the responders' reasoning as to why they think the person's statement is true or false.

Color Cards. Small strips, bits, pieces, and sections of multicolored construction paper are placed in the center of the group. The leader instructs participants to "close your eyes, reflect back over the day's experiences, and try to get in touch with your feelings of this moment. As you do this, try to picture [this is a good exercise for visually oriented people] colors that represent your feelings. Also try to picture if your feelings are big or small, jagged or smooth, linear or round, and so forth. When you open your eyes, select colors and shapes that best match your awareness." The leader then asks group members to explain or describe the pieces of construction paper they have selected.

Medium Intensity

Strength Bombardment. Members individually volunteer to tell what their own personal strengths are, and the group responds by telling what strengths they see in these volunteers. The leader may want to be the first volunteer. The member or leader may extend the exchange by asking. "What do you see as preventing me/you from using those strengths?"

Self-Report. This exercise involves a go-around. Each group member is asked to make a specified number of statements about self, which should be personal: "I am a damned good teacher," "I should be a better parent," "I am feeling overwhelmed by all my responsibilities." The group then reacts. The leader should set the stage by being the first to make the self-report. A variation of this procedure involves use of a timer, such as a small hourglass sand timer. Each member talks about himself or herself during the time allotted.

Metaphors. A catalyst that can be used in the total group or in subgroups (subgroups are a common procedure for early sessions), this activity involves participants forming impressions in their minds of their group mates and trying to associate food, animal, automobile, weather, color, or any item that metaphorically summarizes their impressions. In sharing the metaphor, the most important part is to give the reasoning for the metaphor ("You seem like a teddy bear; you're physically powerful looking but very gentle in disposition"). In this exercise remind the group that responses should if at all possible be positive.

Significant Moment. Members are asked to reflect back in memory to a time, person, or event that proved to have a significant influence on the member's present situation. In accordance with the here-and-now emphasis of extensional groups, the leader tries to help the group use past experiences to stimulate discussion about the member's *present*.

As a Group Member. Toward the end of the group experience, a good activity is to ask members to complete the sentence, "As a group member, I..." This triggers exploration of the meaning of the group for each participant, the commitment he or she has to the group, and perhaps what the member wants or has obtained from the sessions.

Freezing. When group content seems to be drifting off to the there-and-then, the leader might ask members to "freeze" and to elicit feedback from members about their feelings.

Magic Shop. The approach in this activity is to ask members to imagine they can shop at a magic place that stocks only intangibles. Any intangible, such as honesty, love, or great intelligence, may be purchased, but the price is something intangible that the individual already owns—such as good health or joy of living. This is an excellent device to confront group members with their value systems and the commitment each may have to any given set of values. A possible variation is to suggest that members may obtain anything from the Magic Shop but need not return anything. Or they may exchange something they wish to discard for something in the "shop."

Role-Playing. An effective group technique, but one too infrequently used in group counseling, is role-playing. An alert leader can easily find appropriate situations for role-playing arising out of content that group members provide. The technique of role reversal is important, as is sufficient time in the group session to thoroughly explore the implications of the role play. Insights gained through skillful use of this technique usually are highly satisfactory.

High Intensity

Farewell. An excellent exercise for a closing session, this activity permits members to express feelings they have not yet shared. The instructions are: "This is our last session together. Some of us may not see each other again. Take a few minutes to reflect on what messages you would like to leave." Members who have had a meaningful group experience sometimes become quite emotional in doing this exercise. The leader should participate too, but not to the extent that he or she is unavailable to members who are emotional, or to members who may need encouragement to share their farewell messages. A variation of this exercise is to have everyone stand in a circle and express farewells nonverbally as well as verbally. This can be an equally, if not more, emotional experience.

Mirror Image. Group members are asked individually to look at themselves in a mirror (a hand mirror is simple and effective) and describe what they see as honestly as they can. Members then give feedback, agreeing or disagreeing, with reasons given.

Legitimizing. A useful go-around is to ask each member to specify a personal characteristic that he or she feels a need to legitimize. For example, Rick might suggest that he feels his need to manipulate and his need to exert his sexuality may need legitimizing; that is, he feels they are a part of him that is not accepted by others. Group members can give their reactions to the member's quest. Leaders should be alert at this point so that members do not begin "super-mothering" in an effort to legitimize. Super-mothering involves a denial of a member's reality; legitimizing involves complete acceptance and recognition of that member's reality.

Interpersonal Nonverbal Activities

Low Intensity

Line-up. This exercise can be adapted to any theme in which members are looking for nonverbal ways of comparing themselves with group mates. In the initial instruction the members are told that they must stand in a straight line, shoulder to shoulder. They can change their relative positions in the line, but this may cause other members to have to move from their positions. No doubling up in the same spot is permitted. There can be only one person per place. The line may represent a continuum of control—for example, "The people who are at this end of the line are the most controlling group members here, and the one at the very end is admitting that he or she wishes to control *everyone* else in the line." The themes can be love, fearfulness, sexiness—anything that seems relevant to the group's concern of the moment.

Hand Mirroring. As an energizing, enjoyable, nonverbal activity, this one is excellent. It also may produce some interesting dominance-submission insights. Partners stand facing each other with ample room for moving about. They are instructed to put their hands up, palms out, matching each other's palms but not touching. They are to imagine that powerful rubber bands connect their wrists, pulling their palms toward their partner's. *But*, if their palms make contact, they will have completed an electrical circuit that gives them both a painful shock. They can avoid the shock by keeping their palms from touching, but the "rubber bands" keep pulling their palms together. After preliminary instructions, the participants are told to explore their space together—up, down, around. They are also free to move about the room, provided that they remain in the palm-facing-palm position. Some hilarious impromptu dances sometimes result.

Changing Seats. One exercise that can be useful in understanding territorial behavior is for leaders to ask members of a group that has been in session for a time (perhaps a half-hour) to change seats. This can be done by asking the entire group to change places at one time, or perhaps by going around the circle and asking each member in turn to select the place of another member (or leader) as his or her territory. The members should verbalize their reactions to the experience, and the leader should help them see the meanings of their behaviors at whatever level seems appropriate to the maturity and psychological sophistication of the group.

Medium Intensity

Mill-In. This exercise touches the concept of territoriality and has members drift about the room for an unspecified time. The leader deliberately avoids presenting any limits. Eventually each member will establish a "territory," either as part of a subgroup or individually, standing or sitting. How long did it take? How

group lightly massaging and stroking the person's arms or face. All this is done in silence. The person receiving the attention usually prefers to experience it with closed eyes. If the lifted-cradled-rocked-stroked person does not feel that he or she belongs after *this* experience, it is unusual, indeed!

Territoriality. The group is divided in half. One half lines up facing the other across the room. Members extend their arms in front of them and start moving slowly toward the opposite side of the room (a la Frankenstein). They are instructed to take a straight path, and it should lead them to confront someone opposite from them. They will have to decide how to handle the encounter, because they are not permitted to lower their arms or to deviate from a straight path. The resulting discussion usually starts with identifying "cheaters" (people who allow their paths to vary to avoid physically confronting someone from across the room) and invariably gets around to talking about the embarrassment of confronting someone with outstretched arms. Hugging is one natural outcome; others stop, touching hands, unwilling to enter more closely into another's space.

Nonverbal Go-Around. The opportunity for each group member and the leader to communicate nonverbally with all other group members sets the stage for an intense experience. The group leader asks all members to stand up and move into a comfortable, close circle, facing inward, shoulders almost touching. Each member in turn steps into the inner perimeter of the circle and, facing outward, moves from one member to another, attempting to communicate nonverbally his or her feelings for each member. The leader begins this exercise and, thus, sets the tone. The entire exercise is completed in silence. When everyone has had an opportunity to interact with each other, members take their seats and discuss the experience. Most groups find this a deeply moving experience, and the subsequent discussion usually demonstrates increased group solidarity and heightened sensitivity to each other.

Feeling Space. Another exercise in the area of territoriality involves asking group members to close their eyes and explore the space about them while remaining seated or standing and silent. They should be directed to feel down, back, up, to the side. About three minutes should be allotted for this. Leaders should keep their eyes open so that they can observe, making suggestions when necessary. Members commonly "peek," trying to assess what others are doing and how much "safe" space is available. After the activity is over, the leader can gently encourage members to talk about their discomfort at not knowing what is transpiring while their eyes are closed. The *discussion* is far more important than the fact that a member "cheated." The discussion should center on members' reactions, especially those experienced when contact was made with another person, or was not made. How did members feel when they found someone else within their territory? How did they feel about temporary isolation from visual contact? How do they handle isolation elsewhere? What are their solitude needs? What are their companionship needs? How did they feel about making contact with a female? A male? The possibilities for discussion are infinite. Leaders must draw upon their art of group leadership for direction.

Intrapersonal Verbal Activities

Lifeline. Although it is an effective exercise for helping members get better acquainted, this is not appropriate as an introductory activity. Members are to draw a line on a piece of paper, left to right, that reflects the ups and downs of their lives. Afterward, members explain their lines to the others. Listeners are encouraged to ask questions, and presenters are encouraged to elaborate on their lines. It is desirable, sometimes, to break the larger group into subgroups of three to five participants. In this exercise smaller groupings tend to maintain stimulation of interaction, while large groups permit too much anonymity. A variation is to review one's life as a series of critical incidents that stand out in one's memory. On a blank piece of paper each member places a dot on the left-hand side to represent birth. Without lifting the pen or pencil, members depict in graphlike fashion the progress of their lives—the highs, low, and various "in-betweens." Critical incidents in a member's life usually are represented by peaks or valleys in the uninterrupted line. This "road of life" serves as a source for discussion as members share commonalities and differences in their "roads."

Perfect Day. This activity encourages members to share their values and interests in life outside the group. It is also an excellent catalyst for helping members recognize and accept members whose values are different from their own. The instructions are: "All of us have preferences as to how we like to spend our time. But we often have responsibilities that prevent us from doing what we would really like to be doing. If you had the freedom, time, and money to plan a day that is perfect for you, what would it look like?" After they have been allowed quiet time to think, members are given paper and pencil and asked to jot down their thoughts about a perfect day. These thoughts are shared later with the group.

Medium Intensity

Childhood Rediscovery Fantasy. Group members relax and mentally prepare themselves for fantasizing. The leader says, "In your fantasy, recall a particular moment of joy...or sorrow in your childhood. What would you have changed if you had such power? Other childhood rediscovery fantasies might have themes of cleaning out the attic, basement, garage, closet (What do you discover/rediscover?); being in a costume room, free to dress in any manner you choose; or animals in your childhood that you enjoyed/avoided (What was it about them that affected you the way they did?).

Animal Fantasy. Although this exercise can be done quickly, it seems to have the most impact when participants can spend some quiet time thinking about animals they would like to be if reincarnated. In their reflective time, they are to think of the qualities of the animal they admire/respect/detest most.

Autobiographies. The capsule autobiography can be used to effect confrontation. Each group member is asked to write five or six sentences concerning his or her life history. The leader reads these aloud, without identifying the writers. Discussion follows each reading. Is there a life theme (a script)? Group members can gain understanding of the life-space of other group members and may also obtain insight into their own life-space. A focus may also be on future plans. Confrontation will be elicited through this exercise if the group leader is familiar with projective theory.

Symbolic Objects. The leader begins the group by asking each member to select some concrete thing from the environment that symbolizes himself or herself. The area from which to select can be as extensive as time and area allow. When members return to the group, they each present their object and describe how that object symbolizes themselves. The leader should make a selection too and begin the interaction by his or her presentation. For example, the leader might have chosen a set of keys. Then he or she might describe these keys as representing a personal search for answers, always looking for ways to open doors to truth, or looking for ways to unlock relationships with people, or feeling a need for protection or isolation.

What Would You Like to Be Remembered For? In this activity, members explore the memories of themselves that they would like to stand on as their "signatures of essence." This helps participants identify their value structures and the ways in which they are translating those values into action. For instance, one member might want to be remembered for the friends he made, another for the fact that she loved someone very deeply. Some members might not want to be remembered at all. Whatever statements are made can be explored productively.

High Intensity

Gestalt Chairs. This technique is commonly used in gestalt therapeutic approaches. It is normal for an individual to be in conflict between two incompatible situations or conditions. A choice must be made and acted upon, but confusion at having two desirable (or sometimes undesirable) choices seems insurmountable. The person in conflict is asked to sit in one of two chairs and speak from one of the points of view. Then he or she switches to the other chair and speaks from the opposing point of view. When the individual feels that the issue has been thoroughly "debated," he or she elicits feedback from the group.

This is a powerfully effective technique, regardless of the nature of the conflict. It could be as simple as a young man trying to decide about asking a particular girl for a date, or as complex and intense as a young woman deciding whether or not to become a nun.

Twenty-Four Hours to Live. The leader fantasizes that the group has discovered that each member has only the next twenty-four hours to live. The participants in turn describe how they would spend the time.

New Ways of Behaving. For a specified time, group members try out a way of behaving that they consider desirable, but which they have not previously tried. Five minutes may be sufficient for the exercise if the group is not too large. At the end of the designated time, members are asked to report to the group what "new" behaviors they observed in others, to react to their own "new" behavior, and to report the feelings involved. Some members might not be able to identify "new" ways to behave. This realization constitutes an important area for discussion.

Five Roles. Trotzer (1989) describes an activity that is powerful in that it helps members clarify their values as they pertain to many of the most important roles they play in life. It is best used at the beginning of a group and in the early sessions. Each group member is to write five commonly played roles on separate pieces of paper. Give no hint to the group members as to what those roles may be. Once the group members have listed five roles on separate pieces of paper, ask them to decide which role they would be most willing to give up. Ask that the first role to be given up be tossed into the center of the circle. Without discussing the content of the roles retained, members are asked to discuss why they threw the first role away. Continue the cycle, with discussion, until there is only one role left. Some members may not be able to part with more than three roles; others will toss away roles most willingly. When the activity is concluded, have members discuss why they kept the particular role they did and what their feelings were about it. As the discussion proceeds, the leader will likely find many uses for interaction techniques.

Intrapersonal Nonverbal Activities

Low Intensity

Deep Breathing. Deep breathing exercises can be used to open a group session once a group has been taught the technique. It is quite different from the usual process of respiration, which moves air vigorously in and out of the nostrils. The "yoga" approach to deep breathing involves "tuning in" to one's inner world of proprioception and, in particular, to the expansion and contraction feelings of the rib cage that accompany breathing. Members are directed to fill the lower part of their lungs with air first, then the middle part, and finally the upper part. In exhaling, the upper part, then the middle, and then the lower part of the lungs is emptied. The chest remains motionless and passive while the ribs expand during inhalation and contract during exhalation. Members breathe in to the count of four, hold for two counts, and exhale to four counts. Ten or twelve deep breaths are relaxing and help members get in touch with the rib cage and lungs.

Body Relaxation. An exercise that can follow the few minutes of deep breathing involves the leader asking members to sit up straight in their chairs and put both feet flat on the floor, with closed eyes. (In an appropriate setting, this exercise can be done with members lying flat on their backs on the floor.)

The leader then "talks" quietly up the body, beginning with the feet, asking members to relax the muscles in their left foot, then the right foot. Next the leader moves to the left and right lower legs, knees, and so on. This is done slowly, and members' eyes remain closed throughout the entire exercise. The period ends with a few minutes of silence. This procedure allows members to get in touch with their bodies, as well as to relax their muscle systems.

Summary

Structured activities may be useful in encouraging a group to focus on the here-and-now, I and Thou, but the main instrument of movement toward self-growth for the members is the leader. A reasonable amount of interaction is required before the bonds of trust begin to develop among members. The leader's skill, sensitivity, and courage are the major influences in determining success when using the structured exercises presented in this chapter. The reader is reminded of the impossibility of accurately predicting on an a priori basis how effective an activity will be. The site, group purpose, and relative maturity of the group's participants are crucial considerations for determining the "right" activity for the "right" moment.

10

The Extensional Group Model in School Settings

Introduction

Educational settings may be defined in numerous ways. Elementary schools will include grades K through 4, 5, or 6, middle school grades may vary between grades 5 through 8, and high school grades 9 or 10 to 12. Obviously, individual and group characteristics overlap enormously. We have attempted to be sufficiently general to absorb much of the overlap. For that reason, in this chapter we have differentiated between elementary and high school levels only, as it is difficult to define age and grade groups precisely. There has been an attempt to minimize repetition in both levels, as many of the suggestions at the elementary level are adaptable to the high school. Younger aged groups, however, require considerably more preplanned structure than do older groups.

Some group processes are appropriate in elementary or high school, while others are more appropriate in private practice, hospitals, or clinics. For purposes of clarification, group guidance, task-oriented, and small instructional groups are directed toward normal functioning groups, while psychotherapy groups are directed toward persons who are less able to cope with daily functioning and possess less personal ego strength.

Groups specific to elementary and high schools are generally conducted within different parameters from groups outside of schools, not only because schools are usually public institutions dealing with minors but also because young children and adolescents do not possess the ego strength to handle the intense level of interaction characteristic of adult groups. Once young people in their late teens pass through the typical "identity crisis" of that age, the sense of self strengthens, and psychological resources are likely sufficient to benefit from explorations at a deeper level. Until this occurs, however, group leaders must modify their behavior to create group processes appropriate for the young person still in a developmental stage and not psychologically mature.

The extensional group model applied to children still depends heavily on self-disclosure and feedback, but younger members are more dependent on structured activities and prepared materials for achieving interaction. However, this does not mean that younger children cannot interact spontaneously or that older members cannot profit from structured activities.

Types of Groups

In April 1991, the Association for Specialists in Group Work (ASGW) adopted a new set of standards for training group workers. Conyne, Wilson, Kline, Morran, and Ward (1993), in a discussion of the applications of the "standards" in a counselor education training program, defined group work "as a broad professional practice that refers to the giving of help or the accomplishment of tasks in a group setting...by a professional practitioner to assist an interdependent collection of people" (p. 12). They also named the four categories of groups endorsed by ASGW (1992) as follows:

- Task/work groups
- Guidance/psychoeducational groups
- Counseling/interpersonal problem-solving groups
- Psychotherapy/personality reconstruction groups

Using this basic conceptual framework for counselors, Johnson and Johnson (1995) presented a paradigm (see Figure 10.1) that categorizes the various group processes. One category, *content groups,* includes task/work groups and guidance/

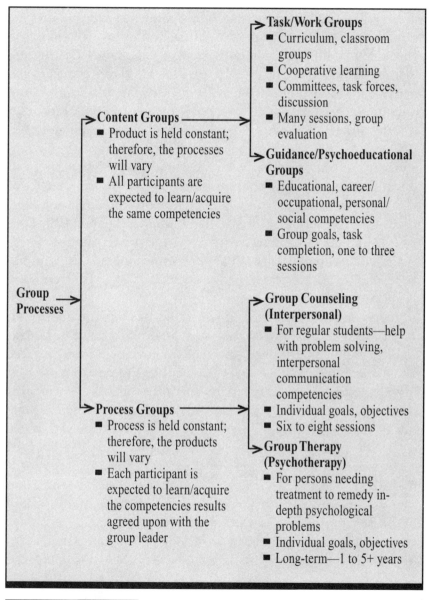

FIGURE 10.1

Categories of Groups

From "Group Process: A Results Approach," by S. K. Johnson and C. D. Johnson, 1995, *Counseling and Human Development, 27*(9), p. 3. Reprinted with permission.

psychoeducational groups; the other category, *process groups,* includes counseling groups (which are used most frequently in school counseling) and therapy groups. Adaptations of the extensional model may be applied to guidance/psychoeducational groups and counseling groups. Both have the aim of assisting students to learn new material, develop specific skills, or alter attitudes toward something or somebody. Johnson and Johnson (1995) advise that guidance/psychoeducational groups and counseling groups are the most misunderstood by the lay public, and educators and even school counselors may suffer from a lack of knowledge of the distinction between them. In delineating their paradigm of group processes, Johnson and Johnson (1995) believe, "When presented and explained, the model should clarify for the general public, students, parents, teachers, and administrators that all these group processes are designed to reinforce learning" (p. 1).

Johnson and Johnson (1995) describe task/work groups (content) as related closely to classroom instruction and organizational work forces. Although counselors may be involved in these groups periodically, classroom teachers use them most often to deliver content curriculum. Administrators use them to facilitate adult-related, faculty, parent, and community functions. Most educators understand the function and purpose of these groups.

On the other end of the spectrum (as described in Chapter 1) are psychotherapy groups that function as personality reconstruction processes. Johnson and Johnson (1995) affirm that "therapy groups are not appropriate within the public school educational program. Even when private mental health resources are scarce, providing therapy groups goes beyond what is legally sanctioned by local and state boards of education" (p. 2).

All the group processes described in Figure 10.1 contribute to learning, and all, to some degree, involve different skills on the part of the group leader. The use of diverse skills depends on the purposes of the group, the setting in which it is conducted, and the composition of group membership. In a guidance/psychoeducational group, the leaders will have in mind information they wish to transmit to the group as a whole. In other words, participants are expected to learn some content, while the dynamics of group interaction are used. There is a group goal whereby students are to acquire similar learning, most of which is primarily in the cognitive domain. In contrast, in a counseling group the leader will emphasize individual goals and focus on individual growth, and leader techniques that emphasize the affective (conative) domain will be in evidence.

Parameters of Learning

The parameters defining the boundaries within which a group operates are governed to some extent by the setting; thus, group leaders must be able to use facilitative techniques suitable for the type of group they are leading.

To achieve guidance group goals, small group activities and small group discussion as well as teaching skills are applicable. The leader will select approaches that best suit the group goals. Discussion techniques, decision-making analysis, simulations, games, multimedia stimuli such as slides, videotapes, and films, role playing, self-assessment procedures, and vocational exploration are some of the common approaches. Problem-centered groups composed of "school attendance problems," "high-risk chemical dependency," "acting-out students," and "divorce groups" may be the focus of content groups. In addition, Johnson and Johnson (1995) explain that groups may include issues of self-esteem, underachievement, conflict resolution, interpersonal relationships, helping peers, making decisions, and handling authority. All of these types are aimed at helping group members cope with the demands of the culture (whether it be the institution or society at large) so they can become functioning and productive citizens.

Fortunately, there is recognition in our society that the individual is also important; that is, a recognition that each individual is unique and in some way different from anyone else, and that these differences are a valuable resource. Enculturation must be effected to some degree before *primary* forces can be focused on individuation, or a society would be in chaos. If *only* enculturation were achieved, society would be changeless.

The *primary* focus of groups where the extensional model is appropriate is to strengthen individual competencies. Members examine their values, priorities, individual strengths, and lifestyles. The content of extensional groups focuses on how members differ one from another and what each can do because of—not in spite of—such differences.

Mixing the Message

Both the learning and individuation processes interweave and are complementary. Therefore, no precise line of demarcation can be drawn between the two processes. The group whose main focus is on learning specific competencies, such as the values, mores, and conventions of society, is obviously different from the group whose focus is on values and behavior that create a unique lifestyle. However, Johnson and Johnson (1995) caution us that mixing the message can create confusion for group members.

> The intentional or unintentional process of mixing content and process groups creates confusion and mistrust in participants. If a group member signs up for a content group or is mandated to attend such a group with the stated expectation of learning a specific skill or attaining information, the participant has a right to feel violated if the group moves into personal and social areas that the individual is unprepared to address. Likewise, an individual seeking a personal growth experience may feel disillusioned if the group turns out to be a process for teaching specific skills that may not apply to the student's individual goals. For example, a student seeking a group experience as a way of exploring life goals may be impacted negatively if the group turns out to be a group designed to encourage students to attend college and provide strategies for how to get into college. In both instances, when groups are misrepresented or if a group evolves from one type of ex-

perience to a different type of group, the long-range impact of the group process may hinder instead of help the individual's progress. (pp. 4–5)

Elementary School Group Counseling

The Purpose

The purpose of elementary school counseling has not changed over time. Both Redl (1966) and Morganett (1994) offer reasons for establishing guidance and counseling groups in the elementary school. Redl (1966) identified areas of application: draining off hostilities and daily frustration so they do not accumulate to an intolerable degree; providing emotional support when children are overwhelmed by feelings of panic or guilt; offering a relationship that keeps the child from retreating into his or her own world as a consequence of emotional upheaval; and serving as a setting in which to work out feelings about disputes, fights, and other matters.

Morganett (1994) describes group work as providing a safe and accepting environment to practice new behaviors and receive the support of others; offering role models for positive attitudes, social values, and behaviors; showing how working together is important and providing models for giving and receiving help; providing a place where children can learn tolerance and respect for others' differences; and providing a place to teach children how to trust and how to share ideas, attitudes, and feelings honestly.

Group counseling with elementary school children is, in essence, no different from counseling in groups with participants of any age, but special considerations must be given to groups composed of elementary school-aged children.

In an elementary school-aged counseling group, it is important to preserve the integrity of the home and family, and the leader must be alert to assure that the young student does not discuss issues that would violate this privacy. Elementary school children cannot be expected to have the degree of social so-phistication older students will have; thus, the leader must vig-orously protect each child's privacy as well as that of their fami-lies. This may involve more frequent intervention than is usu-ally necessary when working with an older group.

Composing the Group

The method of developing a counseling group (at any grade level) should not be left to chance. The composition of a group may be of great importance to the kind of group life that will de-velop and the effects the group will have on its members. Among elementary school students, the possibilities of contagion (mean-ing "one bad apple will spoil the barrel") are greater than they are when students are older. Therefore, children ought not be put into a group where they do not belong, as they will either seriously disturb the group or will suffer damage through expo-sure to the wrong group life. Redl (1966) believes that students should be somewhat homogeneous in respect to toughness, physi-cal prowess, sexual sophistication, and developmental stage. If a leader finds that a student has been misplaced in a counseling group, the leader should confer with the student privately and remove the student from the group. Of course, it must be made clear to the student that there will be an opportunity to meet on an individual basis with the counselor. Students, regardless of age and sophistication, must not feel they are abandoned when removed from a group.

Some special considerations must be observed when orga-nizing and conducting counseling groups composed of elemen-tary school children. The size of the group and the length of each session depend on the ages of the children. For example, in early childhood (ages 5 through 9) the group should contain only three or four members who meet no longer than 20 to 30 minutes at one time. Not every child is ready for a group, and children should be selected in such a way that overactive or ag-gressive children are not grouped together. One such child per group is sufficient. Of course, as suggested earlier, there are other examples of a "poor mix."

Leaders who work with elementary school groups find that they must do more "teaching" of listening skills, membership skills, and individual behavior than would be necessary or desirable in older age groups. Children need a great deal of help in labeling emotions, as well as in articulating their value systems. Positive emotional development in children is analogous to self-actualization in adults.

Communication Patterns

Group leaders who work from an existentialist framework with the extensional model find that the principles and procedures of enhancing communication as advanced in this book are appropriate when working with groups of all ages. Children of elementary school age, however, have limitations in communication. They are not as practiced at verbalizing feelings as are older students. And even more than older students, they tend to respond with "it" type comments—facts, events, and things away from the group that deal with the there-and-then. Children also tend to make "they" responses. They will focus on people away from the group rather than deal with each other. Thus, young students need help with the skills that stimulate genuine communication. A leader should be alert to these types of responses and may either model more productive interaction or discuss ways of interacting directly.

As an example, young students usually "chain" at first; they respond to one another's comments with replies that indicate no verbalized recognition of the content of the other's remarks. For instance, David, a group member, might state that he had a bad fight with his sister. A chaining response might be, "I just have a new sister in my house. She's really neat!" This type of response chains to the output but gives the previous speaker no indication that his comment held meaning for the receiver. Elementary school children particularly need to be helped to make associative responses as well as to give feedback.

In the associative response, the child will give some recognition that he or she has heard the speaker but centers the response geocentrically. Taking David's comment about the fight with his sister, the child might reply, "Yeah, I know what you mean. I fight with my sister sometimes." This type of response leaves the original speaker with some small degree of satisfaction, but the feedback has only been minimal. He was heard, but does not know if he was understood.

A group leader's task is to assist the group member to add to the associative response some meaningful feedback that contains some affect. Affective responses require a high degree of listening skills; this is one of the functions of the group process—to help members learn to listen to each other. The feedback level of response centers on what the speaker is saying, responds to it, and enriches it. This kind of response is "interactive" in that it enables the dialogue to move back and forth between two people rather than reaching a dead end. In responding to the comment about fighting with a sister, a feedback response might be, "I have fought with my sister, and it isn't a nice feeling." All group participants have some difficulty in learning to give this sort of feedback, but elementary school students have a particular struggle in learning how to communicate at a level in which they transmit "hearing" feelings.

So far we have discussed the extensional group model as it pertains to counseling. Elementary school classroom groups (guidance/psychoeducational groups) are more topically oriented than are counseling groups. Factors to be considered in elementary school groups, particularly those at the youngest levels, are that considerably more structure and preplanning of activities are necessary in comparison to groups of older children. Puppets (Dinkmeyer & Dinkmeyer, 1982), "magic circle" (Bessell & Palomares, 1970), classroom meetings (Glasser, 1975), openended stories (Morganett, 1990, 1994), role plays, and art work are suggested activities for young children's groups.

Goals for Classroom Group Activities

Typical goals of classroom group activities include:

- Achieving a curriculum or instructional goal
- Helping new students get acquainted
- Problem solving
- Demonstrating democratic principles
- Increasing confidence to participate in discussions
- Clarifying values

When students enter a newly formed class, they wonder, "What's this teacher going to be like?" "What are my classmates going to be like?" "Are they going to be smart? tough? friendly?" Teachers are usually concerned about their students' personal uncertainties and curiosities about their class members. It would take very little time away from instructional objectives for a teacher, using a group approach, to attend to these natural concerns of students.

School children spend a lot of their time in groups of some kind as part of their educational experience. In the classroom setting, group activities tend to be highly structured as compared with other types of group settings. The teacher is usually the primary influence on the content of discussion and controls the directions taken by the group. We believe that classroom group leaders (teachers) can utilize certain elements of the extensional model to be more effective in performing their duties. We hasten to emphasize that we are proposing the extensional model as an *adjunct* to the traditional role of the teacher and certainly not as a replacement of any existing educational model.

Values are formed, and protocols of behavior are established, that are as distinctive as they are implicit. Such micro-societies are inevitable in any classroom. Good teachers are aware that these micro-societies have an important influence on students' achievement and attitudes. The influence can be positive or negative, and even when teachers are aware of the class social structure, they may be uncertain about what to do to contribute to its healthy development. Extensional group-type activities can serve as a vehicle for influencing the positive development of the classroom's micro-society, and thus improve its educational and emotional climate.

The statement above is based on two assumptions: First, we assume that students learn more efficiently when they are personally involved in the learning process. Second, we assume that peers are extremely influential in affecting student attitudes and behaviors. When students can be accepting of themselves, they are more likely to be accepting of others. Only when they function well within their peer group will they be able to attain the utmost of their potentials. We would expect, therefore, greater achievement with comparatively less effort in an educational environment where positive interaction among peers is built into the curriculum, and where students are encouraged to explore and examine their feelings about themselves, their classmates, and their educational experiences.

Resources for Elementary School Classroom Groups

As mentioned previously in this chapter, we are convinced that group work should be considered in a broader context than just counseling—for example, guidance and psychoeducational groups. The distinction between group counseling and classroom group discussion is sometimes obscure. Their purposes differ, and *counseling* usually calls for a departure from the normal classroom routine. But the process of interpersonal contact, speaking spontaneously in the here-and-now, and receiving feedback is just as important to a skilled teacher as it is to a skilled group leader. Both of them are, in reality, group facilitators. Whereas group leaders may focus *entirely* on the interactive process of the group participants, classroom teachers call upon their awareness and group leadership functions at times when they think their students' learning can be positively effected.

The literature directed to group activities for elementary school classroom groups is limited in comparison with the literature focusing on human relations training, older adolescent groups, and adult groups. Morganett (1990, 1994) has developed two excellent books of activities for the use of teachers and counselors. The earlier publication is for those working with young adolescents and includes group activities for what she calls "group agendas," dealing with topics such as "Meeting, Making and Keeping Friends," and "Better Ways of Getting Mad: Anger Management Skills." Her second volume includes "agendas" for group experiences with children from the second to the fifth grade. A sampling of the agendas are, "I'm Somebody Special: Building Self-Esteem," "Friends: Getting Along with Others," "Kids in Divorce Stress," and "I'm Responsible." How materials such as these are used depends on leader emphasis and the group setting. Morganett's (1994) "Houndie and Mutsy" (see Appendix 10A, page 181) is offered as a sample of a structured activity available to classroom teachers and counselors. Following the story, which is to be read to the children, is a series of questions to assist the classroom teacher with group interaction.

High School Group Counseling

The Adolescent Dilemma

Leading a group of young people involves strategies and an organization that differs significantly from those employed for adults and young children. The tumultuous world of the adolescent is fraught with experiences unlike those of adults, which in turn creates an enigmatic haze around their attitudes and behavior. Adolescents are constantly in the process of change— change in body image, change in mood, change in emotions as a result of hormonal development, and change in thinking and patterns of response to events in their lives. As a result of these turbulent changes, adolescents in groups are apt to be more cunning in dealing with their adult leaders and will create interpersonal barriers, often displaying ongoing resistance with a vigor that will test the patience of most leaders.

Adolescence is also a period when young people eagerly experiment with adult behavior and attitudes while gradually relinquishing the securities of childhood. It is an exciting yet, at times, frightening period of growth for many teenagers. Adults who attempt to advise and counsel young people through this transition period are often more impressed with the wisdom of their guidance than are the recipients. The values and experience gap between adults and adolescents can be sizable and, as a result, frustrating to adults who are genuinely trying to be of help. Nevertheless, it is no less frustrating and confusing to teenagers who are seeking a sense of self-identification in which they feel competent, independent, and accepted among peers. This is a common adolescent concern, although the intensity of the concerns and confusion varies considerably. Adolescents are most likely to turn to their peers in search of answers and support. In their bid for independence and self-identification, most teens are particularly conscious of the peer-relevant mores and values that are in vogue.

Acceptance by peers is significantly more important to high school students than are the opinions and advice of adults. Among adolescents, what is acceptable and unacceptable by teen standards is known by all and is constructed and imposed by the students themselves. Simply stated, students decide that some aspects of their existence are "safe" to share. Other interests, thoughts, and aspirations that they might genuinely wish to share are not shared because students suspect they would be ridiculed or rejected by volunteering them. Involvement in almost any variety of sporting activity is preferable to and "safer" than speaking with pride about beekeeping. Sharing the excitement of a weekend party is less risky than describing the excitement of a book read over the weekend.

In many classrooms peer influence can develop an insidious character. For whatever reasons, some students are judged by their peers to be not "with it" by contemporary peer standards. Even if these individuals are not patently ostracized, they are often intentionally "not noticed."

Students spend a good part of their school day in some form of group activity—committees, task-oriented classroom groups, and so on. Most often, though, group interaction takes place in casual gatherings in the classroom, corridors, cafeteria, and after school.

It has already been proposed that group interaction offers the potential for growth and positive change, and since young people are in groups anyway, why doesn't this potential emerge naturally? One of the basic reasons it does not emerge naturally is that teenagers typically are beginning to monitor their behavior, how they dress, what they say, and so forth. The proclivity toward fads and conformity is probably the most obvious verification that teens are concerned, to varying degrees, about how they are perceived by others. In their peer consciousness, teens are beginning to manifest characteristics to protect themselves from possible peer rejection. In high school, students with a weak self-identity or poor self-concept typically are concerned about behaving as they think they ought to rather than as they are. Many high school students have difficulty revealing themselves authentically, and often what looks spontaneous is really a facade. Other students appear bored and sullen because that is the image they wish to convey.

It can be assumed that young people have serious thoughts and concerns that they would like to communicate to others. Unfortunately, many educational settings do not encourage this type of interaction. Adolescents' natural strengths and resources can be channeled and shared for mutual benefit if a sensitive and knowledgeable adult (group leader, teacher, counselor) is available to facilitate interaction. Since peer influence is such a pervasive force among teens, we should capitalize on its power for constructive purposes. The school climate and instructional efficiency would be improved if such opportunities were made available. The abilities of teachers and counselors can be utilized in structuring group situations in which students may share their opinions and perceptions. This may lead to confrontation between students or between students and teachers, but confrontation can be constructive. Frequently, a peer confrontation includes the same information with which an adult might confront the student. The main difference is the identity of the confronter. Our hypothesis is simple: It is more difficult for an adolescent to reject or deny the opinions of a peer than those of an adult. The feelings expressed by peers seem to have more impact.

The following examples indicate the importance of peer interaction. Imagine the following statements being made to adolescents by an adult. Then imagine the same interaction between adolescents.

- I really think you have a lot to be proud of. You're attractive and intelligent.
- You don't bore me. I think you have had many interesting experiences.
- I think you're blowing it. You look strung out all the time.
- You always act so hard. You don't need to act that way. I don't think you are really that way at all.

These examples are excerpted from student comments made in actual high school group counseling sessions. If teachers were to say the same things to students, however, the statements would probably be rejected as being "your values, not mine." If a student makes the same kind of statement to another student, it stands a better chance of being heard and considered. Consequently, the group leader should try to develop and maintain an environment designed to maximize listening and assimilation of the information and opinions being shared among adolescents.

The extensional group model seems to be an ideal vehicle for focusing on interaction that is honest, spontaneous, and positive. Group leaders do not prohibit feedback that is negative or calculated, but they are careful not to permit continued negative feedback intended to be destructive or vindictive. Leaders can use negative feedback in the group process to influence authentic, positive interaction. Extensional group techniques, however, are not designed or employed for evoking negative confrontations. Our approach to the group process centers on capitalizing on positive feedback.

Learning and personal growth are maximized when we feel good about ourselves and when we have confidence in the support and acknowledgment of our peers. When inviting adolescent members into a group, counselors can acknowledge the potential of a group member. After receiving an invitation, a parent called the counselor to inquire, "What's wrong with my son?" The counselor replied, "We're inviting your son to participate because there is something he can contribute to the group. The reason he was invited to join wasn't because there is something wrong with him!"

Each group member is unique. Each group leader is unique. The extraordinary qualities of individual members and individual leaders make each group unpredictable to some degree. The complexities that comprise the entity called "group" are so intricate that they defy definition and, therefore, anticipation. Experienced and inexperienced leaders alike approach each group as an unknown. Perhaps a major difference between experienced leaders and inexperienced leaders is that the former know they can never be sure what will evolve in a group and the latter still believe that, in time, they might.

Getting Organized

Morganett (1990) recommends the following procedures when organizing a group experience for students:

1. *Conduct a needs assessment.* Find out what group services are needed by the students in a particular setting.
2. *Develop a written proposal.* After need has been established, develop a proposal detailing what you are going to do, and how you are going to do it.

3. *Advertise the group.* See "Staff Preparation" and "Presentation to Students."
4. *Obtain informed consent from parent/guardian if this is school policy.* This involves providing specific information about the group so that the parent/guardian can make an intelligent decision about whether or not to participate (see Appendix 10B, page 187).
5. *Conduct a pre-group interview.* Talk to the student about your expectations as well as their expectations (what their interests might be) of the group. See "Pre-Group Interview."
6. *Select group members.* Specific guidelines are detailed elsewhere in this chapter.
7. *Conduct post-group follow-up and evaluation.* This is essential for accountability for reporting to administrators, teachers, or parents. See "Accountability."

Goals and Objectives

Educational goals that can be achieved through the use of group counseling in public schools are a legitimate concern of school counselors. Bates (1968) conducted research to identify which of those goals could be achieved through group processes when working with adolescents in a high school setting. According to her study, group counseling could be used to help students become more receptive to the learning process through the reduction of tension and hostilities. In one group format of her study, students were helped to maintain a grade-point average, improve behavior in the classroom, demonstrate more applied effort, and increase daily attendance. Students in the groups expanded the occupational choices into which they projected themselves, and these chosen occupations were more realistic when assessed against the student's academic potential.

It is unrefuted that the goals and objectives that can be achieved through group counseling are consonant with the goals and objectives of education. In the extensional model, leaders assist prospective group members in identifying the goals and objectives that each wishes to achieve. A group leader's goals might include the young person's ability to improve interpersonal skills and develop self-management strategies, problem-solving techniques, and active coping skills. The criteria for group membership is directed toward individuals within a "normal" population who, with the help of the group, can attain such goals.

Staff Preparation

The typical high school staff probably misunderstands the purpose of group to a greater extent than does any other institution. Counselors who wish to initiate group counseling will likely find their time in staff preparation well spent. Without the staff's understanding and support, almost any group counseling program will encounter difficulty.

First of all, the administrators' support *must* be obtained—not just permission, but support, preferably enthusiastic support. If an administrator gives only lukewarm agreement, counselors may want to delay the group counseling program until they are able to elicit clearer understandings on the part of administrators of the educational advantages of a group counseling program.

After the support of the administration has been gained, a general presentation concerning the nature of group counseling, its values, and educational components should be made to the faculty. At this point, it is recommended that the building administrator express support of the group counseling program to the entire faculty.

Defining Membership

The first step in working with young people in a group is to define criteria for membership. The best group member is a self-referred group member; group counseling should be optional for participants. Among adolescents it is advisable to exclude those whose behavior is so bizarre that other group members will be frightened or whose behavior is beyond the mores of acceptance for group members. Other unsuitable candidates include withdrawn or passive individuals and those who are so troubled that they spill their anxieties at an uncontrollable pace. Particular combinations of group members also may cause problems. For instance, a group should not be put together to benefit one person; benefits derived in group work are for the group as a whole. If the group bogs down and members drop out, inadequate choice in membership is most often the cause. Finally, in composing a group, leaders should take into consideration the degree to which each of the participants is verbal; too few or too many highly verbal members may inhibit group interaction. Two relevant questions asked by Corey and Corey (1992) are: (1) Is the group suitable for the individual, and (2) is the individual suitable for the group?

With respect to grade level and same-sex or mixed-sex groups, there is really no hard and fast rule. No significant body of research suggests that young people function more productively with peers of the same grade level or with the same sex. Yet, as a general practice, it is best to form groups according to grade level when working in a school setting. Not only are developmental issues a consideration, but the social events and behavioral expectations of students also vary as they move from grade to grade.

Group progress may be hampered if students are too divergent in age or development. With older adolescents, however, mixed-sex groups are generally preferred. Young people in grades 6 through 8 usually work better in single-sex groups as pre-teen boys are unpredictable in their behavior and their loyalty to the opposite sex. Single-sex groups are better able to work on understanding these inconsistencies. The developmental stages of both boys and girls can have a troublesome effect on the group.

Pre-Group Interview, Group Size, Number, and Length of Sessions

The usual size for an adolescent group is seven or eight, which allows for dropouts. Once a group falls below five members, the dynamics change and the group becomes less productive.

The school-based extensional group model suggests that leaders schedule a pre-group interview, eight group counseling sessions, and a post-group interview. Thus, a counseling group can be organized, conducted, and evaluated within the framework of a school quarter. If the pre-group interview is done well, and if the group leaders are skilled, eight sessions should be sufficiently productive. The notion of continuing one group for a semester or a year (or two!) in the public school setting is neither necessary nor desirable.

If a leader believes an individual group member should continue working in a group, the member can be reassigned, and thus not be denied the opportunity for continuance. At the same time, each of the group members will have had the experience of working with a limited number of sessions and may have internalized a basic fact of living—that opportunities (and life) have limits.

Usually the group meets weekly for one class period. Meeting for the same period each week is best, but if leaders work in a traditionally scheduled school, they may elect to rotate the periods for group meetings (first period first week, second period second week, and so on). In a modular scheduled school, groups can meet when the student has free time, but it is suggested that no groups be organized before or after school or during the lunch hour. If counseling is a legitimate part of the educational program, time ought to be available for group counseling as well as classroom instruction.

Once the group has been informed of the number of weeks it is scheduled to meet, the group's life should not be extended. If the need arises to extend the duration beyond the contracted period of time, Carroll and Wiggins (1997) suggest leaders might ask themselves, "Have I helped group members recognize that meeting individual goals is not strengthened by endless participation? Am I fostering dependency by continuing the group?"

During the time the group meets, no new members should be added. Achieving group cohesiveness within the established number of meetings is important to provide the emotional security needed for members to explore new growth experiences. Because counseling groups have an established, limited number of meetings, allowing changes in membership hinders the formation of group cohesiveness (Johnson & Johnson, 1995).

When considering the length of individual group meetings, groups move more productively when there is a known beginning and a known end. Time limits should be set not only for the number of weeks the group is to meet but also for the length of the individual sessions. Above all, adhering to specific time limits is important for consistency. It cannot be overemphasized that groups move more productively when there is a time frame for each session and a known number of weeks the group will meet. Consistency is imperative for adolescents.

Seating Arrangement

Does the place where group members choose to sit have any significance? The answer is yes and no. Carroll and Wiggins (1997) believe that the leader should avoid making interpretations in regard to who sits where. Of course, certain hypotheses can be drawn, and these can be tested as the group proceeds. More important, though, the leader should watch for neurotic pairings, such as adolescents who pair off by sitting next to each other in every session and whisper, continually nudge each other, and snicker periodically. Leaders can separate such pairs in a way that does not seem negative or uncaring. One possibility is for the leader to attempt to sit between the pairs, as subtly as possible, as the pairs attempt to sit together in the group. It is important to remember that separating problem members can be essential to the life of the group.

Logistics

If possible, a group should meet in other than a classroom setting. Privacy should be maximum, with no interruptions permitted. Chairs should be arranged in a circle, not around a table.

The leader must begin on time, even if only one member is present. The session also must end on time. Beginning group leaders tend to want to extend the time of their sessions, as groups led by beginners characteristically get down to work toward the end of a session. If neophyte leaders allow the time to be extended, they are denying group members the opportunity to learn limits and therefore to gain experience in reality testing.

Special Considerations

When high school counseling groups begin to acquire the potential for intense interaction of the type that is observed among adult groups, some special concerns may arise. Examining long-term values, assuming personal responsibility, planning for the future, understanding sexuality, clarifying self-identification, and getting along with parents and authority figures are issues that do not normally emerge in groups of younger children but are common in adolescent groups.

Because of the potential for "heavy" issues, the group leader should have a clear picture of why group counseling seems appropriate and desirable for his or her particular group of high school students. Being absolutely clear on this point is a requisite for enlisting the support and understanding of the faculty and administration.

Communication Patterns of Adolescents: What to Look For

The range of and gaps in social and communication skills seem more pronounced among adolescents, particularly those in their early teens, than among any other age group. Interaction with members of the opposite sex is often awkward. Preoccupation with status, age, and grade-level differences can interfere with clear and sincere communication. Even sustaining normal eye contact is a problem for some teens. In short, adolescence is a time of relative uncertainty about oneself, demonstrated sometimes by social clumsiness and difficulty with clear, personal articulation.

Understanding the developmental and transitory personality aspects of adolescence can guide group leaders in their efforts to help members express themselves openly and to learn from their experience with other teens. The awkwardness observed in many adolescents requires, perhaps, more leader vigilance for encouragement and support than for other types of groups.

A communication pattern that lingers from pre-teen days is difficulty with conscious self-disclosing in the here-and-now and the tendency not to listen to group mates. This statement is a generalization about teens, and adults are certainly not immune to such group behavior. But the pattern seems to be more noticeable among adolescents, partly because of their self-consciousness and partly because schools rarely encourage the kind of interaction that is encouraged in group.

What a teen may intend to be self-disclosure is frequently an impersonal narrative, as if the teen were describing himself or herself as a character in a movie or TV script, through phrases like, "and I go...," "and she said...," "and then *I* said...," "and she goes..." Personalizing pronouns as a part of speaking directly about oneself is foreign to most adolescents, as well as to most adults. Instead of saying "I" or "my" when referring to themselves, they tend to detract from the intensity of a personal statement by saying, "you," "it," "we," "us." "Ya know" and "OK?" are examples of "filler-phrases" that mean nothing in themselves but may give adolescents the feeling that they have added substance to their statements. These detractions are not used consciously to avoid deeper, more personal interaction; they are speech habits developed over time. Speech patterns are copied, just as music and clothing styles are copied.

Consider the following dialogue taken from a group session with high school freshmen:

> *Paula:* ...and my name comes blaring over the intercom, ya know..."Paula C., please report to the vice principal's office..." and I go, "Oh, no! (rolling her eyes) Not again!"...OK...and then, ya know what? The teacher, she goes, "PAULA, did you hear your name?"...and I go, "If he wants to see me, why doesn't he come here?"...just kidding, ya know...and the class cracks up laughing...OK...Well, she gets mad, ya know, and starts yelling her lungs out...ya know.
>
> I mean...ya know...ya kinda get embarrassed when your name comes blaring over the intercom...that's a bummer, ya know...cheez, everybody in school knows you're in trouble...ya know...and then, having this teacher screaming like a banshee...ya know...and it was just a little joke...OK. It's like a prison around here...OK...and the teachers are like guards...ya know.

The leader's task in extensional group is to help Paula focus on speaking personally and to distinguish between the description of an historic event and the feelings she might be experiencing about it in the present.

Another communication pattern to which all groups are subject, but one that is particularly noticeable among adolescents, is the tendency not to really listen to each other. They may *hear* the words spoken by another, but they do not understand or empathize. For example, in the statement above, while Paula is talking about her experience, nonlisteners are recalling when they got called to the vice principal's office, and if they respond in the group they will likely narrate their experiences. "Story telling" is a common communication pattern in adolescent groups, and a leader must work to rechannel it to more productive here-

and-now interaction. "Story telling" is never a here-and-now expression.

Presentation to Students

If possible, it is suggested that the group leader make presentations in the classroom to introduce students to the program. At this time it is important to avoid using group pressure to stimulate individual interest. The leader does not ask students to indicate an interest in joining a counseling group at this time. Instead, after explaining the purpose of the group, a pamphlet (see Appendix A, page 201) can be given to the students. In addition, students must be informed as to how they can contact the counselor. This may be in the form of a personal visit to the counselor's office, leaving one's name in a box outside the office, or any other unique way the counselor can suggest to allow students to make a contact.

Counselors should consult with the administration, informing them of procedures, objectives, and potential benefits of the group counseling program; with the support of administration, counselors can then inform faculty and parents.

Checklist for Organizing School Counseling Groups

Finally, when the leader feels that all preparations are complete, a checklist can be useful as a quick reference.

	Yes	No
1. Did you clear with administration and faculty?	____	____
2. Have you made a general presentation to students in the classroom setting? (optional)	____	____
3. Have you selected the potential members?	____	____
4. Do you have permission slips (if school policy requires) prepared for parents to sign?	____	____

5. Are students of all one grade level? _____ _____
6. Are students of the same sex (or mixed)
   depending upon grade level? _____ _____
7. Did you clearly explain to each student
   his or her membership responsibility? _____ _____
8. Is everyone in the school (administration, faculty, and students participating)
   aware of time limits, location, and
   number of sessions? _____ _____
9. Are you assured of uninterrupted privacy
   in the setting you will use? _____ _____
10. Do you know how you are going to
    follow-up or evaluate the group sessions? _____ _____

Accountability

According to Carroll and Wiggins (1990), leaders have to be accountable to themselves as they seek to improve, and to others as they try to demonstrate that time and effort spent in group work is worthwhile. Leaders cannot depend on the research completed by others; that research doesn't address the groups they are leading or their effectiveness as leaders. So each leader is personally responsible for proving that his or her efforts result in measurable benefits to group members. Carroll and Wiggins suggest a five-step model demonstrating accountability:

1. Setting goals
2. Assessing current status
3. Planning interventions
4. Evaluating outcomes
5. Reporting results (pp. 79–83)

Setting Goals

What does the leader—or the group—want to have happen as a result of the group process? The leader may determine these goals and either share them with group members or simply keep them in mind as a desirable outcome. For example, a leader may have this goal: "For my clients to have a higher internal locus of control as a result of going through this group experience." This implies that clients will become more independent and less influenced by group opinion as a result of group inter-actions. Another possible goal would be to raise measured self-esteem on a pre-group and post-group (pre-post) basis. The possibilities are many and varied.

Assessing Current Status

Prior to starting counseling, the leader may want to determine the current functioning levels of group members. Many locus of control and self-esteem instruments are available for use as needs assessment measures for members. They could be admin-istered to all members at the first session or to each member individually when selecting group members.

Other needs assessment methods of a less formal nature may include pre-post testing of member concerns, completion of adjective checklists describing oneself, very formal assessments using personality inventories administered by third parties, the use of logs or diaries subjected to leader critiques, and many other possible methods. For example, Carroll and Wiggins (1990) have used Rotter's Internal-External Locus of Control instru-ment (Rotter, 1966) on a pre-post-post basis with groups to first determine pre-group status, then a second test six weeks after the group completed its meetings to determine changes leading to more internal locus of control, and a final testing six months after that to see if positive changes were maintained.

For younger groups, the Self-Esteem Inventory (Coopersmith, 1967) has been used to see if the post-test scores were corre-lated with group interventions. Also, teacher behavior ratings on a pre-post basis have been correlated with improved behav-ior after group work has been completed.

Planning Interventions

After goals have been set and an assessment of needs completed, the leader has to decide if a specific type of intervention is needed to help reach the listed goals.

Leaders should also attempt to determine if their specific types of interventions work. Do group members truly have improved self-esteem, a higher internal locus of control, or receive more favorable ratings by external observers after the group intervention? If so, can these be improved even more? If not, is it because of leader skills, poor selection of members, or other reasons? The purpose of evaluation is to demonstrate success or to help plan for changes that will lead to success.

Evaluating Outcomes

For group leaders who are not concerned with rigorous research, the pre-group and post-group assessment will be sufficient to accomplish their purpose—evaluating an individual member's progress. The perennial problem that has clouded the results of studies of the effectiveness of group work will need to be faced however. *If* a group mean statistic is used, the basic stance that a group does not have a group goal but only individual objectives for each individual member is contradicted. A gain for one group member may be a loss for others; therefore, leaders who do research must be prepared to state individual hypotheses for each of their subjects if they are to remain consistent. The fact that this complicates research procedures is recognized. The leader is obligated to become familiar with the abundant literature on groups in which different (desired) directions in movement of individual members canceled out statistical significance.

Reporting Results

Most organizations require results of the evaluations to be submitted to administrators and other decision makers. Notwithstanding the research problems of the validity of self-report instruments, criterion problems, and statistical significance, some form of evaluation is better than none.

Summary

An important aspect of the extensional group model is that teachers can instigate it, can be involved in the activity themselves, and can control it for educational purposes. Group counseling, however, is to be provided by a trained professional school counselor. Counselors are cautioned that educators may object to using valuable educational time to encourage students to get to know each other and themselves better, particularly if structured activities are used exclusively as part of the extensional group process and are perceived as "games."

Counselors would be prudent to look at their own accountability in group work. Setting goals, assessing the current status of members, planning interventions, evaluating outcomes, and reporting results are methods by which a leader can show responsibility to administrators. It is part of the professional leader's responsibility to show there has been an attempt to help others change in positive ways. In addition, accountability allows the group leader to build a resource base for the future.

Appendix 10A
Structured
Teacher Activity

Houndie and Mutsy

In the home of Rosi and Phillip Jefferson lived two dogs named Houndie and Mutsy. Houndie was a beautiful Afghan hound, with flowing, silky hair and ears and a curled-up tail like a monkey's. She was so beautiful that people would stop Rosi and Phillip when they were out walking the dogs and ask what kind of dog she was. They would say things like "Oh, that dog is so regal, she looks like a queen."

Now Mutsy, who was no special kind of dog at all, just kind of hung back and followed on the walks, looking very dejected and sad indeed when this happened. In fact, Mutsy was joked about and called an "arf" dog, for "arf terrier" and "arf everything else!" This was a joke because it sounded like "half and half." Poor Mutsy—nobody said he was beautiful or regal or even cute. In fact, Mutsy had an unusual way of walking because his leg had been broken when he was just a tiny puppy, and it had grown together crooked. So Mutsy walked with a sway and a hitch and dragged his leg a little, making him look even more discombobulated!

One day after their walk, Mutsy and Houndie were talking to each other, the way dog friends do. Mutsy said, "Houndie, I think the world of you as my best friend, and I know you like me very much, too. But when we are on walks with Rosi and Phillip and people say nice things to you and mean things to me, I feel like crying, like getting angry at them and chewing their shoes, like saying 'Hey, notice how pretty my markings are, and that I have an excellent nose,' but I don't—I just stand there and cry to myself. Would you be willing to stick up for me and not take all of the attention, and pay attention to how I feel? I like myself just how I am, and I need to know my friends accept me for who I am, too, not how pretty or ugly I am."

Houndie didn't realize that her friend Mutsy felt so terrible, awful, and horrible about being teased and discounted by the kids and grown-ups in the neighborhood. She said, "Oh, Mutsy! I'm sorry! I haven't been a very good friend to you. I haven't been loyal to your friendship because I forgot you when you needed me. I like for people to say how pretty I am, and I didn't realize that you need people to see that you have many special things about you, too, even though they aren't on the outside. I want everyone to know that being different on the outside does not mean that you are not beautiful on the inside. You are the most loving, loyal, honest, and special friend I have ever had. I will try hard to be more aware of your feelings and to appreciate you."

The next day, Phillip and Rosi took the dogs for their walk. Houndie pranced in her high-stepping style, and Mutsy came along behind, dragging his leg a little, but with a friendly attitude in his heart. The neighbors were working in their yard and said to Phillip and Rosi, "Oh, my, Houndie is such a gorgeous creature!" Houndie knew they were saying lovely things about her beauty. She tossed her head and stepped highly, her long hair flowing. She looked like the queen of the desert. Houndie looked back at Mutsy, who was staring down. She knew he must be feeling rejected and ugly. She ran to him and whispered in dog language in his ear, "Mutsy, it looks as though you feel rejected and unappreciated because those people don't know what a beautiful dog you are inside. I do. And I appreciate all of you."

Mutsy realized that he was not going to be able to change the opinion of some people about his looks, but he felt very proud of his friendship with Houndie. He could ask for things he needed, he could tell Houndie his true feelings, and she would listen to his ideas and make him feel special for who he was, not what he looked like on the outside. Mutsy knew that he and Houndie had a very special friendship!

Help children respond to the following questions:

- What to you think Mutsy felt like when he was called names and rejected by people in the neighborhood? Have you ever felt this way?
- What did Mutsy do about getting the positive feelings he needed and the recognition for who he was inside? How could you do something like that?
- Can you change other people's feelings and thoughts?
- Can you change your own feelings and thoughts?
- After Mutsy asked Houndie to pay attention to his feelings and his true self, she watched and listened to him to know how he was feeling. Who could you watch and listen to so you could let them know you understand?
- What kind of feelings and recognition are important in friendship?
- How do you feel when you share your feelings with your friends?

Source: From *Skills for Living: Group Counseling Activities for Young Adolescents* (pp. 47–48) by R. S. Morganett, 1990, Champaign, IL: Research Press. Copyright 1990 by R. S. Morganett. Reprinted by permission.

Appendix 10B
Letter to Parents

Letter to Parents

**Elementary Guidance Department
Hubbardston Center School**

Dear Parents/Guardians,

One of the services offered at Hubbardston Center School is small group counseling. Groups are formed and designed around the needs of the individual students, which can vary from year to year.

Groups are typically made up of four to six students who get together on a weekly basis for approximately six to ten weeks. Depending on the age of the children, each group session meets for about thirty to forty minutes. Developmental issues such as friendships, peer pressure, stress, and transition to middle school are covered, as well as life change issues like death, moving, and divorce.

Referrals for small groups come from teachers, parents, and students. If you are interested in finding out more information, return the form below or give me a call at _____.

I look forward to hearing from you.

Sincerely,

Naida Johnson
School Counselor

I would like more information about small groups being offered at Hubbardston Center School. Please give me a call at _____.

Signature _____

A Member of the Quabbin Regional School District

This letter was reprinted with permission from the Quabbin Regional School District.

Training Issues

The Basics

The executive board of the Association for Specialists in Group Work adopted an expanded version of the *Professional Standards for the Training of Group Workers* in April 1991. To date there is minimal evidence that graduate training programs follow the ASGW (1992) standards. Indeed, there has been little change in the attitudes of faculty trainers since Yalom first declared in 1985 (1995) that "many training programs for mental health professionals are based on the individual therapy model and either do not provide group therapy training or offer it as an elective part of the program. In fact, it is not unusual for students to be given excellent intensive individual therapy supervision and then, early in their program, be asked to lead therapy groups with no specialized guidance whatsoever" (p. 512).

A decade later Corey (1995) stated, "For proficient learners to emerge, a training program must make group work a priority. Unfortunately, in some master's programs in counseling not even one group course is required, and in others such a course is still an elective. In those programs that do require course work in group counseling, there is typically one course that covers both the didactic and experiential aspect of group process" (p. 44). Thus, there is still concern about the quality of group training. ASGW's (1992) efforts have not gone entirely unheeded, however. The Council for Accreditation of Counseling and Related Educational Programs (CACREP) have adopted a number of the

ASGW (1992) standards. Unfortunately, there are too many institutions training mental health counselors in group work who fail to seek CACREP accreditation.

Requirements and Objectives for Group Course Work

Course work for core training in group work should include at least one basic course in groups, which provides information about group work, group development, leader and member roles, group dynamics, and outcome evaluation (Conyne et al., 1993). Objectives for core course work in group work include (but are not limited to) identifying and describing the following:

- The nature of group counseling, its advantages and disadvantages, its facilitative forces, and when it is indicated and contraindicated
- The distinguishing characteristics of major approaches to group counseling and the commonalities among them
- Normal human development as related to group counseling
- Individual and interpersonal assessment in group counseling
- Principles of group formation for group counseling
- Interpersonal and intrapersonal dynamics in group counseling
- Standard methods of intervention in group counseling
- Use of referral sources in group counseling
- Methods for evaluating group counseling
- Ethical considerations unique to group counseling (p. 15)

We will now take a closer look at the four specialized groups defined by the ASGW (1991) standards and examine the competencies group leaders should exhibit when working with these groups.

Task/Work Groups

Definition. Group workers who specialize in promoting the development and functioning of task and work groups seek to assist such groups to enhance or correct their function and performance. Task and work group specialists use principles of group dynamics, organizational development, and team building to enhance group members' skills in group task accomplishment and group maintenance. The scope of practice for these group work specialists includes normally functioning individuals who are members of naturally occurring task or work groups typically functioning within an organizational context. (Conyne et al., 1993, p. 16)

Within task/work groups the process of decision making and the awareness of the responsibility for the decisions are experienced by those involved. Face-to-face discussion with airing of opposing views and opinions is encouraged. The dynamics of problem solving, trial-and-error experiences, and the skills of committee work such as reaching a consensus through discussion are implicit in the dynamics of task/work groups. The dynamics of brainstorming may be used to encourage creativity among the participants. Members may learn group skills such as gatekeeping, harmonizing, initiating, clarifying, informing, summarizing, reality testing, compromising, and consensus testing.

Training requirements. The type of training given to teachers, personnel workers, and organizational development workers in their professional education should be supplemented by some specialized knowledge of the dynamics of task group processes. Personality characteristics, such as the ability to tolerate some confusion and patience with the democratic process, should enable the leader to function adequately in these small activity groups.

Guidance/Psychoeducational Groups

Definition. Education and prevention are critically important goals for the contemporary counselor. The psychoeducational group specialist seeks to educate group participants who are normally functioning individuals who may be informationally deficient in some area, perhaps because of inadequate family or cultural teachings about how to cope with external threats, developmental transitions, or personal and interpersonal crises. The scope of practice of psychoeducational group leaders includes essentially normally functioning individuals who are "at risk" for but currently unaffected by an environmental threat (e.g., AIDS), who are approaching a developmental transition point (e.g., new parents), or who are in the midst of coping with a life crisis (e.g., suicide of a loved one). The overarching goal in psychoeducational group work is preventing future development of debilitating dysfunction. (Conyne et al., 1993, p. 17)

In part a didactic approach may be used in group guidance/psychoeducational groups, including multimedia presentations. Frequently, a paper and pencil instrument, which might include an interest inventory or a diagnostic instrument of study skills, is used to provide background for discussion. Small group discussion is included as well as face-to-face discussions, verbalizations of attitudes and values surrounding the content materials, questions and answers, role playing, panel discussions, and sociodrama.

Training requirements. Teaching skills are basic, but the leader of a guidance group also needs to possess a body of specialized technical knowledge concerning educational and vocational areas as well as group dynamics. This training is usually obtained through course work in an institution of higher learning offering an approved program of counselor education.

Counseling Groups

Definition. The group worker who specializes in group counseling seeks to help group participants to resolve the usual, yet often difficult, problems of living by stimulating interpersonal support and group problem solving. Group counselors help participants to develop their existing interpersonal problem-solving competencies so that they may be better able to handle future problems of a similar nature. The scope of practice of group counselors includes nonsevere career, educational, personal, interpersonal, social, and developmental concerns of essentially normally functioning individuals. (Conyne et al., 1993, p. 18)

The group counselor deliberately establishes an unstructured field so as to use tensions that arise from ambiguity. Thus, members bring to the group concerns that have root in the affective domain. The group leader uses techniques of reflection of both ideas and feelings, clarifies distortions and contradictions, may or may not summarize, links ideas and feelings, listens intensely for surface and subsurface meanings, may encourage confrontation, and generally focuses on the value systems of participants as they are reflected in life choices. The leader provides an experience where members can test limits through specifying a limited number of sessions—from six to eight—which begin and end on time.

Training requirements. The leader should have specialized training in leading counseling groups, which includes supervised group leadership. A certification of competency in group counseling leadership should be obtained from an institution of higher learning offering an approved program of counselor education.

Psychotherapy Groups

Definition. The specialist in group psychotherapy seeks to help individual group members remediate in-depth psychological problems or reconstruct major personality dimensions. The group psychotherapist differs from specialists in task/work groups, psychoeducational groups, or counseling groups in that the group psychotherapist's scope of practice is focused on individuals with acute or chronic mental or emotional disorders that evidence marked distress, impairment in functioning, or both. (Conyne et al., 1993, p. 19)

Psychotherapy groups are usually organized for the purpose of correcting severe behavior disorders that impede an individual's function. The purpose may be a major or minor restructuring of personality. Approaches will vary depending on the theoretical orientation of the leader.

Training requirements. Training for leading therapy groups is highly specialized and usually long term; also, training requires an advanced degree. Personal therapy on the part of the leader, both individual and group, are often prerequisite to entering training as a group therapy leader.

Beyond Formal Training

Improving Competence

From an ethical perspective it is imperative that counselors seek constant upgrading of skills. Carroll and Wiggins (1997) suggest the following paths for counselors who seek ongoing professional development.

1. Pursue additional group experience as a participant. Although a person may have had group experience in a higher institution training program, it is imperative to have additional post-training group experience.
2. Find a mentor who will assist with ongoing supervision.
3. Attend training institutes, workshops, and in-service programs to upgrade skills. Consult professional association newsletters for notices of in-service programs.
4. Remain up to date by staying current with the professional literature.
5. Develop a pattern for self-reflection; one should examine one's own motives and issues when doing group work.
6. Develop a theoretical base for your counseling that will provide you with a consistent pattern for group leadership.
7. Join professional organizations such as the Association for Specialists in Group Work (ASGW) or the American Group Psychotherapy Association (AGPA).

Credentialing Agencies

The following credentialing agencies maintain certification for professional practice.

- National Board of Certified Counselors (NBCC)
  3 D Terrace Way
  Greensboro, North Carolina 27403

- National Council for Credentialing of Career Counselors
  c/o NBCC (see address under NBCC)

- American School Counselor Association
  801 North Fairfax Street, Suite 310
  Alexandria, Virginia 22314
  (credentialing: c/o NBCC)

- National Academy for Certified Clinical Mental Health
  Counselors
  801 North Fairfax Street, Suite 304
  Alexandria, Virginia 22314

- Commission on Rehabilitation Counselor Certification
  162 North State Street, Suite 317
  Chicago, Illinois 60601

- American Association for Marriage and Family Therapy
  1717 K Street, N.W., Suite 407
  Washington, D.C. 20006

- American Psychological Association
  1200 Seventeenth Street, N.W.
  Washington, D.C. 20036

- American Group Psychotherapy Association, Inc.
  25 East 21st Street, 6th Floor
  New York, New York 10010

Summary

The four basic categories of group work have been defined according to the Association for Specialists in Group Work *Professional Standards for the Training of Group Workers* (1992).

Training requirements for each of the four categories of group work are described and advice for ongoing professional development has been suggested. Finally, a list of professional credentialing agencies is given for those who wish information on specific certification requirements in a particular discipline of the professional groups listed.

Training, development, growth, practice, and experience are all essential and yet all didactic in nature. Only the creativity, insight, and affirmation of the individual leader can bring a sense of essence to the group experience. Leadership and the internalization of process must be honed.

Appendix A
Purpose of Group
Counseling

So You Are Going to Be in Group Counseling:
An Induction Tool for Students

To the Student:

This pamphlet was written to help answer some of your questions about group counseling. You will find included some questions that have been asked by other students concerning group counseling which may be helpful in explaining how you will fit in group counseling. You may have other questions or thoughts to discuss so please feel free to ask your counselor.

What Is Group Counseling?

Group counseling can mean many things to many people, but it provides an opportunity to:

  1. talk about common concerns or problems
  2. express your feelings in a small group
  3. help you to understand how you are seen by others.

How Often Do We Meet?

The group will meet at least one period a week for a number of weeks that your counselor has suggested. Meetings will begin on time and end on time.

Who Is Going to Be in the Group?

We will have at least one counselor and 5 to 10 other students who have expressed an interest in discussing their feelings, goals, and other interests. The group members may be all girls, all boys, or sometimes both. Students are usually in the same grade.

What Can I Gain by Being in a Group?

1. You may come to understand others in the group more clearly.
2. This understanding of others can help you to see and evaluate yourself more clearly.
3. You may gain an understanding of your strengths and benefit from these.
4. It gives you a place to express yourself and your feelings.
5. You may find you have concerns similar to others in the group and realize that you are not alone.

What Will Be Expected of Me?

Some of the things the group would expect of you:

1. to be there on time
2. to be honest
3. to be willing to listen to the others
4. to be willing to respond to others

Do I Have to Be in the Group?

No, but we would like you to be if you want to.

Can I Quit the Group?

You may leave the group any time you wish to do so.

Would You Like to Reserve a Place? _____

Your Objectives:

Thanks is given to Al Finlayson, Counselor, Orange Unified School District, Orange, California, for his permission to use this pamphlet.

Appendix B
Ethical
Guidelines

Ethical Guidelines for Group Counselors

Preamble

One characteristic of any professional group is the possession of a body of knowledge, skills, and voluntarily, self-professed standards for ethical practice. A Code of Ethics consists of those standards that have been formally and publicly acknowledged by the members of a profession to serve as the guidelines for professional conduct, discharge of duties, and the resolution of moral dilemmas. By this document, the Association for Specialists in Group Work (ASGW) has identified the standards of conduct appropriate for ethical behavior among its members.

The Association for Specialists in Group Work recognizes the basic commitment of its members to the Ethical Standards of its parent organization, the American Association for Counseling and Development (AACD) and nothing in this document shall be construed to supplant that code. These standards are intended to complement the AACD standards in the area of group work by clarifying the nature of ethical responsibility of the counselor in the group setting and by stimulating a greater concern for competent group leadership.

The group counselor is expected to be a professional agent and to take the processes of ethical responsibility seriously. ASGW views "ethical process" as being integral to group work and views group counselors as "ethical agents." Group counselors, by their very nature in being responsible and responsive to their group members, necessarily embrace a certain potential for ethical vulnerability. It is incumbent upon group counselors to give considerable attention to the intent and context of their actions because the attempts of counselors to influence human behavior through group work always have ethical implications.

The following ethical guidelines have been developed to encourage ethical behavior of group counselors. These guidelines are written for students and practitioners, and are meant to stimulate reflection, self-examination, and discussion of issues and practices. They address the group counselor's responsibility for providing information about group work to clients and the group counselor's responsibility for providing group counseling services to clients. A final section discusses the group counselor's responsibility for safeguarding ethical practice and procedures for reporting unethical behavior. Group counselors are expected to make known these standards to group members.

Ethical Guidelines

1. *Orientation and Providing Information:* Group counselors adequately prepare prospective or new group members by providing as much information about the existing or proposed group as necessary.

   ■ Minimally, information related to each of the following areas should be provided.

   (a) Entrance procedures, time parameters of the group experience, group participation expectations, methods of payment (where appropriate), and termination procedures are explained by the group counselor as appropriate to the level of maturity of group members and the nature and purpose(s) of the group.

   (b) Group counselors have available for distribution a professional disclosure statement that includes information on the group counselor's qualifications and group services that can be provided, particularly as related to the nature and purpose(s) of the specific group.

(c) Group counselors communicate the role expectations, rights, and responsibilities of group members and group counselor(s).

(d) The group goals are stated as concisely as possible by the group counselor including "whose" goal it is (the group counselor's, the institution's, the parent's, the law's, society's, etc.) and the role of group members in influencing or determining the group's goal(s).

(e) Group counselors explore with group members the risks of potential life changes that may occur because of the group experience and help members explore their readiness to face these possibilities.

(f) Group members are informed by the group counselor of unusual or experimental procedures that might be expected in their group experience.

(g) Group counselors explain, as realistically as possible, what services can and cannot be provided within the particular group structure offered.

(h) Group counselors emphasize the need to promote full psychological functioning and presence among group members. They inquire from prospective group members whether they are using any kind of drug or medication that may affect functioning in the group. They do not permit any use of alcohol and/or illegal drugs during group sessions and they discourage the use of alcohol and/or drugs (legal or illegal) prior to group meetings that may affect the physical or emotional presence of the member or other group members.

(i) Group counselors inquire from prospective group members whether they have ever been a client in counseling or psychotherapy. If a prospective group member is already in a counseling relationship with another professional person, the group counselor advises the prospective group member to notify the other professional of their participation in the group.

(j) Group counselors clearly inform group members about the policies pertaining to the group counselor's willingness to consult with them between group sessions.

(k) In establishing fees for group counseling services, group counselors consider the financial status and the locality of prospective group members. Group members are not charged fees for group sessions where the group counselor is not present and the policy of charging for sessions missed by a group member is clearly communicated. Fees for participating as a group member are contracted between group counselor and group member for a specified period of time. Group counselors do not increase fees for group counseling services until the existing contracted fee structure has expired. In the event that the established fee structure is not appropriate for a prospective member, group counselors assist in finding comparable services of acceptable cost.

2. *Screening of Members:* The group counselor screens prospective group members (when appropriate to their theoretical orientation). Insofar as possible, the counselor selects group members whose needs and goals are compatible with the goals of the group, who will not impede the group process, and whose well-being will not be jeopardized by the group experience. An orientation to the group (i.e., ASGW Ethical Guideline #1) is included during the screening process.

■ Screening may be accomplished in one or more ways, such as the following:

(a) Individual interview,

(b) Group interview of prospective group members,

(c) Interview as part of a team staffing, and

(d) Completion of a written questionnaire by prospective group members.

3. *Confidentiality:* Group counselors protect members by defining clearly what confidentiality means, why it is important, and the difficulties involved in enforcement.

(a) Group counselors take steps to protect members by defining confidentiality and the limits of confidentiality (i.e., when a group member's condition indicates that there is clear and imminent danger to the member, others, or physical property, the group counselor takes reasonable personal action and/or informs responsible authorities).

(b) Group counselors stress the importance of confidentiality and set a norm of confidentiality regarding all group participants' disclosures. The importance of maintaining confidentiality is emphasized before the group begins and at various times in the group. The fact that confidentiality cannot be guaranteed is clearly stated.

(c) Members are made aware of the difficulties involved in enforcing and ensuring confidentiality in a group setting. The counselor provides examples of how confidentiality can non-maliciously be broken to increase members' awareness, and help to lessen the likelihood that this breach of confidence will occur. Group counselors inform group members about the potential consequences of intentionally breaching confidentiality.

(d) Group counselors can only ensure confidentiality on their part and not on the part of the members.

(e) Group counselors video or audio tape a group session only with the prior consent and the members' knowledge of how the tape will be used.

(f) When working with minors, the group counselor specifies the limits of confidentiality.

(g) Participants in a mandatory group are made aware of any reporting procedures required of the group counselor.

(h) Group counselors store or dispose of group member records (written audio, video, etc.) in ways that maintain confidentiality.

(i) Instructors of group counseling courses maintain the anonymity of group members whenever discussing group counseling cases.

4. *Voluntary/Involuntary Participation:* Group counselors inform members whether participation is voluntary or involuntary.

(a) Group counselors take steps to ensure informed consent procedures in both voluntary and involuntary groups.

(b) When working with minors in a group, counselors are expected to follow the procedures specified by the institution in which they are practicing.

(c) With involuntary groups, every attempt is made to enlist the cooperation of the members and their continuance in the group on a voluntary basis.

(d) Group counselors do not certify that group treatment has been received by members who merely attend sessions but did not meet the defined group expectations. Group members are informed about the consequences for failing to participate in a group.

5. *Leaving a Group:* Provisions are made to assist a group member to terminate in an effective way.

   (a) Procedures to be followed for a group member who chooses to exit a group prematurely are discussed by the counselor with all group members either before the group begins, during a pre-screening interview, or during the initial group session.

   (b) In the case of legally mandated group counseling, group counselors inform members of the possible consequences for premature self-termination.

   (c) Ideally, both the group counselor and the member can work cooperatively to determine the degree to which a group experience is productive or counterproductive for that individual.

   (d) Members ultimately have a right to discontinue membership in the group, at a designated time, if the predetermined trial period proves to be unsatisfactory.

   (e) Members have the right to exit a group, but it is important that they be made aware of the importance of informing the counselor and the group members prior to deciding to leave. The counselor discusses the possible risks of leaving the group prematurely with a member who is considering this option.

   (f) Before leaving a group, the group counselor encourages members (if appropriate) to discuss their reasons for wanting to discontinue membership in the group. Counselors intervene if other members use undue pressure to force a member to remain in the group.

6. *Coercion and Pressure:* Group counselors protect member rights against physical threats, intimidation, coercion, and undue peer pressure insofar as is reasonably possible.

   (a) It is essential to differentiate between "therapeutic pressure" that is part of any group and "undue pressure," which is not therapeutic.

   (b) The purpose of a group is to help participants find their own answer, not to pressure them into doing what the group thinks is appropriate.

   (c) Counselors exert care not to coerce participants to change in directions that they clearly state they do not choose.

   (d) Counselors have a responsibility to intervene when others use undue pressure or attempt to persuade members against their will.

   (e) Counselors intervene when any member attempts to act out aggression in a physical way that might harm another member or themselves.

   (f) Counselors intervene when a member is verbally abusive or inappropriately confrontive to another member.

7. *Imposing Counselor Values:* Group counselors develop an awareness of their own values and needs and the potential impact they have on the interventions likely to be made.

   (a) Although group counselors take care to avoid imposing their values on members, it is appropriate that they expose their own beliefs, decisions, needs, and values, when concealing them would create problems for the members.

   (b) There are values implicit in any group, and these are made clear to potential members before they join the group. (Examples of certain values include:

expressing feelings, being direct and honest, sharing personal material with others, learning how
to trust, improving interpersonal communication,
and deciding for oneself.)

(c) Personal and professional needs of group counselors are not met at the members' expense.

(d) Group counselors avoid using the group for their
own therapy.

(e) Group counselors are aware of their own values
and assumptions and how these apply in a
multicultural context.

(f) Group counselors take steps to increase their
awareness of ways that their personal reactions to
members might inhibit the group process and they
monitor their countertransference. Through an
awareness of the impact of stereotyping and dis-
crimination (i.e., biases based on age, disability,
ethnicity, gender, race, religion, or sexual prefer-
ence), group counselors guard the individual rights
and personal dignity of all group members.

8. *Equitable Treatment:* Group counselors make every reasonable effort to treat each member individually and
equally.

(a) Group counselors recognize and respect differences
(e.g., cultural, racial, religious, lifestyle, age, disability, gender) among group members.

(b) Group counselors maintain an awareness of their
behavior toward individual group members and are
alert to the potential detrimental effects of favor-
itism or partiality toward any particular group
member to the exclusion or detriment of any other
member(s). It is likely that group counselors will
favor some members over others, yet all group
members deserve to be treated equally.

(c) Group counselors ensure equitable use of group time for each member by inviting silent members to become involved, acknowledging nonverbal attempts to communicate, and discouraging rambling and monopolizing of time by members.

(d) If a large group is planned, counselors consider enlisting another qualified professional to serve as a co-leader for the group sessions.

9. *Dual Relationships:* Group counselors avoid dual relationships with group members that might impair their objectivity and professional judgment, as well as those which are likely to compromise a group member's ability to participate fully in the group.

(a) Group counselors do not misuse their professional role and power as group leader to advance personal or social contacts with members throughout the duration of the group.

(b) Group counselors do not use their professional relationship with group members to further their own interest either during the group or after the termination of the group.

(c) Sexual intimacies between group counselors and members are unethical.

(d) Group counselors do not barter (exchange) professional services with group members for services.

(e) Group counselors do not admit their own family members, relatives, employees, or personal friends as members to their groups.

(f) Group counselors discuss with group members the potential detrimental effects of group members engaging in intimate inter-member relationships outside of the group.

(g) Students who participate in a group as a partial course requirement for a group course are not evaluated for an academic grade based upon their degree of participation as a member in a group. Instructors of group counseling courses take steps to minimize the possible negative impact on students when they participate in a group course by separating course grades from participation in the group and by allowing students to decide what issues to explore and when to stop.

(h) It is inappropriate to solicit members from a class (or institutional affiliation) for one's private counseling or therapeutic groups.

10. *Use of Techniques:* Group counselors do not attempt any technique unless trained in its use or under supervision by a counselor familiar with the intervention.

(a) Group counselors are able to articulate a theoretical orientation that guides their practice, and they are able to provide a rationale for their interventions.

(b) Depending upon the type of an intervention, group counselors have training commensurate with the potential impact of a technique.

(c) Group counselors are aware of the necessity to modify their techniques to fit the unique needs of various cultural and ethnic groups.

(d) Group counselors assist members in translating in-group learnings to daily life.

11. *Goal Development:* Group counselors make every effort to assist members in developing their personal goals.

(a) Group counselors use their skills to assist members in making their goals specific so that others present in the group will understand the nature of the goals.

(b) Throughout the course of a group, group counselors assist members in assessing the degree to which personal goals are being met, and assist in revising any goals when it is appropriate.

(c) Group counselors help members clarify the degree to which the goals can be met within the context of a particular group.

12. *Consultation:* Group counselors develop and explain policies about between-session consultation to group members.

(a) Group counselors take care to make certain that members do not use between-session consultations to avoid dealing with issues pertaining to the group that would be dealt with best in the group.

(b) Group counselors urge members to bring the issues discussed during between-session consultations into the group if they pertain to the group.

(c) Group counselors seek out consultations and/or supervision regarding ethical concerns or when encountering difficulties that interfere with their effective functioning as group leaders.

(d) Group counselors seek appropriate professional assistance for their own personal problems or conflicts that are likely to impair their professional judgment and work performance.

(e) Group counselors discuss their group cases only for professional consultation and educational purposes.

(f) Group counselors inform members about policies regarding whether consultations will be held confidential.

13. *Termination from the Group:* Depending upon the purpose of the participation in the group, counselors pro-

mote termination of members from the group in the most efficient period of time.

(a) Group counselors maintain a constant awareness of the progress made by each member and periodically invite the group members to explore and reevaluate their experiences in the group. It is the responsibility of group counselors to help promote the independence of members from the group in a timely manner.

14. *Evaluation and Follow-up:* Group counselors make every attempt to engage in ongoing assessment and to design follow-up procedures for their groups.

(a) Group counselors recognize the importance of ongoing assessment of a group, and they assist members in evaluating their own progress.

(b) Group counselors conduct evaluation of the total group experience at the final meeting (or before termination), as well as ongoing evaluation.

(c) Group counselors monitor their own behavior and become aware of what they are modeling in the group.

(d) Follow-up procedures might take the form of personal contact, telephone contact, or written contact.

(e) Follow-up meetings might be with individuals, groups, or both to determine the degree to which: (i) members have reached their goals, (ii) the group had a positive or negative effect on the participants, (iii) members could profit from some type of referral, and (iv) as information for possible modification of future groups. If there is no follow-up meeting, provisions are made available for individual follow-up meetings to any member who needs or requests such a contact.

15. *Referrals:* If the needs of a particular member cannot be met within the type of group being offered, the group counselor suggests other appropriate professional referrals.

    (a) Group counselors are knowledgeable of local community resources for assisting group members regarding professional referrals.

    (b) Group counselors help members seek further professional assistance if needed.

16. *Professional Development:* Group counselors recognize that professional growth is a continuous, ongoing, developmental process throughout their careers.

    (a) Group counselors maintain and upgrade their knowledge and skill competencies through educational activities, clinical experiences, and participation in professional development activities.

    (b) Group counselors keep abreast of research findings and new developments as applied to groups.

Safeguarding Ethical Practice and Procedures for Reporting Unethical Behavior

The preceding remarks have been advanced as guidelines that are generally representative of ethical and professional group practice. They have not been proposed as rigidly defined prescriptions. However, practitioners who are thought to be grossly unresponsive to the ethical concerns addressed in this document may be subject to a review of their practices by the AACD Ethics Committee and ASGW peers.

    ■ For consultation and/or questions regarding these ASGW Ethical Guidelines or group ethical dilemmas, you may contact the chairperson of the ASGW Ethics Committee. The name, address, and telephone number of the current ASGW Ethics Committee Chairperson may be acquired by telephoning the AACD office in Alexandria, Virginia, at (703) 823-9800.

■ If a group counselor's behavior is suspected as being unethical, the following procedures are to be followed:

(a) Collect more information and investigate further to confirm the unethical practice as determined by the ASGW Ethical Guidelines.

(b) Confront the individual with the apparent violation of ethical guidelines for the purposes of protecting the safety of any clients and to help the group counselor correct any inappropriate behaviors. If satisfactory resolution is not reached through this contact, then:

(c) A complaint should be made in writing, including the specific facts and dates of the alleged violation and all relevant supporting data. The complaint should be included in an envelope marked "CONFIDENTIAL" to ensure confidentiality for both the accuser(s) and the alleged violator(s) and forwarded to all of the following sources:

1. The name and address of the Chairperson of the state Counselor Licensure Board for the respective state, if in existence.

2. The Ethics Committee, c/o The President, American Association for Counseling and Development, 5999 Avenue, Alexandria, Virginia 22304

3. The name and address of all private credentialing agencies that the alleged violator maintains credentials or holds professional membership.

Approved by the Association for Specialists in Group Work (ASGW) Executive Board, June 1, 1989.

References

Allen, G. (1968, January). Hate therapy—sensitivity training for planned change. *American Opinion.*

Anderson, S. C. (1968). Effects of confrontation by high-and-low-functioning therapists. *Journal of Counseling Psychology, 15,* 411–416.

Anglund, J. W. (1970). *A slice of snow.* New York: Harcourt, Brace, Jovanovich.

Association for Specialists in Group Work (1991). Professional standards for training of group workers. *Together, 20,* 9–14.

Association for Specialists in Group Work: Professional standards for training of group workers (rev.) (1992). *The Journal for Specialists in Group Work, 17*(1).

Bates, M. (1968). A test of group counseling. *Personnel and Guidance Journal,* 749–753.

Bates, M., & Johnson, C. D. (1969, March) The existentialist counselor at work. *The School Counselor,* 245–250.

Benjamin, A. (1978). *Behavior in small groups.* Boston: Houghton Mifflin.

Bessell, H., & Polomares, U. (1970). *Methods in human development.* San Diego: Human Development Training Institute.

Bowers, W., & Gauron, E. (1981). Potential hazards of the co-therapy relationship. *Psychotherapy: Theory, Research and Practice. 18,* 225–228.

Bugenthal, K. F. T. (1965). *The search for authenticity.* New York: Holt, Rinehart & Winston.

Carroll, M. R., & Wiggins, J. (1990). *Elements of group counseling: Back to the basics.* Denver: Love Publishing.

Carroll, M. R., & Wiggins, J. (1997). *Elements of group counseling: Back to the basics* (2nd ed.). Denver: Love Publishing.

Conyne, R., & Wilson, F. R., Kline, W. B., Morran, D. K., & Ward, D. E. (1993). Training group workers: Implications of the new ASGW training standards for training and practice. *The Journal for Specialists in Group Work, 18*(1), 12–19.

Coopersmith, S. (1967). *The antecedents of self-esteem.* San Francisco: W. H. Freeman.

Corey, G. (1995). *Theory and practice of group counseling* (4th ed.). Pacific Grove, CA: Brooks/Cole.

Corey, G., & Corey, M. S. (1992). *Groups process and practice* (3rd ed.). Pacific Grove, CA: Brooks/Cole.

Corey, G., Corey, M. S., & Callanan, P. (1993). *Issues and ethics in the helping professions* (4th ed.). Pacific Grove, CA: Brooks/Cole.

Dinkmeyer, D., & Dinkmeyer, D., Jr. (1982). *Developing understanding of self and others* (D-2). Circle Pines, MI: American Guidance Service.

Dreyfus, E. A. (1962). Counseling and existentialism. *Journal of Counseling Psychology, 9*(2), 128–134.

Dyer, W. W., & Vriend, J. (1980). *Group counseling for personal mastery.* New York: Sovereign.

Fast, J. (1971). *Body language.* New York: Pocket Books.

Friedman, W. H. (1989). *Practical group therapy.* San Francisco: Jossey-Bass.

Gans, R. (1962). Group co-therapists and the therapeutic situation: A critical evaluation. *International Journal of Group Psychotherapy, 12,* 82–88.

Glasser, W. (1975). *Schools without failure.* New York: Harper.

Grotjahn, J., Kline, F. M., & Friedmann, M. C. (1983). *Handbook of group therapy.* New York: Van Nostrand Reinhold.

Ivey, A. E., Normington, C. J., Miller, C. D., Morrill, W. H., & Hasse, R. R. (1968). Microcounseling and attending behavior: An approach to prepracticum counselor training. [monograph supplement]. *Journal of Counseling Psychology, 15,* 5.

Johnson, S. K., & Johnson, C. D. (1995). Group process: A results approach. *Counseling and Human Development, 27*(9), 1–8

Kierkegaard, S. (1944). *Concepts of the dead* (translated by Walter Lowrie). Princeton: Princeton University Press.

Knapp, M., & Hall, J. (1992). *Nonverbal communication in human interaction* (3rd ed.). Fort Worth: Harcourt Brace.

Kottler, J. A. (1986). *On being a therapist.* San Francisco: Jossey-Bass.

Kottler, J. A. (1994). *Advanced group leadership.* Pacific Grove, CA: Brooks/Cole.

Krieg, F. J. (1988). *Group leadership training and supervision manual for adolescent group counseling in schools* (3rd ed.). Muncie: Accelerated Development.

Lewin, K. (1935). *A dynamic theory of personality.* New York: McGraw-Hill.

Lieberman, M. A., Yalom, I. D., & Miles, M. B. (1973). *Encounter groups: First facts.* New York: Basic Books.

Luft, J. (1963). *Group processes: An introduction to group dynamics.* Palo Alto, CA: Mayfield.

McMahon, & Links, P. S. (1984). Cotherapy: The need for positive pairing. *Canadian Journal of Psychiatry, 29,* 385–389.

Morganett, R. S. (1990). *Skills for living: Group counseling activities for young adolescents.* Champaign: Research Press.

Morganett, R. S. (1994). *Skills for living: Group counseling activities for elementary students.* Champaign: Research Press.

Morris, V. C. (1966). *Existentialism in education.* New York: Harper.

Passons, W. R. (1975). *Gestalt approaches to counseling.* New York: Holt, Rinehart & Winston.

Powell, J. (1969). *Why am I afraid to tell you who I am?* Chicago: Argus Publications.

Redl, F. (1966). *When we deal with children.* New York: Free Press.

Rotter, J. B. (1966). Generalized expectancies of the internal vs. external control of reinforcement. *Psychological Monographs*, (80).

Russell, A., & Russell, L. (1980). The uses and abuses of co-therapy. *Advances in Family Psychiatry, 2,* 401–410.

Schutz, W. C. (1967). *Joy: Expanding human awareness.* New York: Grove.

Schutz, W. C. (1977). *FIRO-B* (2nd ed.). Palo Alto: Consulting Psychologists Press.

Shapiro, J. L. (1978). *Methods of group psychotherapy & encounter.* Itasca: Peacock.

Shulman, L. (1979). *The skills of helping.* Itasca: Peacock.

Siu, R. G. H. (1968). *The man of many qualities—A legacy of the I Ching.* Cambridge: MIT Press.

Trotzer, J. P. (1989). *The counselor and the group* (2nd ed.). Muncie: Accelerated Development.

Wallen, J. (n.d.). *The constructive use of feelings.* Beaverton, OR: Tektronix, Inc.

Wolfgang, A. (1985). The function and importance of nonverbal behavior in intercultural counseling. In G. Corey, M. Corey & P. Callanan (Ed.), *Issues and ethics in the helping professions* (4th ed.) (p. 255). Pacific Grove, CA: Brooks/Cole.

Yalom, J. D. (1995). *Theory and practice of group psychotherapy* (4th ed.). New York: Basic Books.

Index